DEEP COVER

Burt Rapp

DEEP COVER
DEEP COVER
DEEP COVER
DEEP COVER
DEEP COVER

Police Intelligence Operations

PALADIN PRESS
BOULDER, COLORADO

Deep Cover:
Police Intelligence Operations
by Burt Rapp
Copyright © 1989 by Burt Rapp

ISBN 0-87364-507-3
Printed in the United States of America

Published by Paladin Press, a division of
Paladin Enterprises, Inc., P.O. Box 1307,
Boulder, Colorado 80306, USA.
(303) 443-7250

Direct inquiries and/or orders to the above address.

Contents

Preface

The purpose of this handbook is to inform and instruct the police officer, police administrator, and his ultimate boss, the citizen and taxpayer. All need to know just what *intelligence* is, what purpose it serves, and exactly how police officers gather and use it. And, most important, all need to know what intelligence can and cannot do.

The individual police officer needs to know all this because he often has something to contribute to police intelligence gathering. He may serve in the intelligence bureau one day, and this handbook will provide an orientation for that job. He also needs to know why he has to provide certain reports and other types of information for other officers he doesn't know and may never see. Knowing the end-use will help the officer do a better job of gathering and recording seemingly unimportant information.

The police administrator who was never exposed to a

competent intelligence operation needs to know how and why it works. He may need an intelligence bureau in his department, but have no idea how to set one up. If such a unit already exists, the administrator may misunderstand it and not know how to direct or evaluate the bureau's activities. He may feel the officers are doing an excellent job, when in fact they're unproductive. Alternately, he may wrongly perceive the officers within as lazy or incompetent. Make no mistake about it: A poorly planned or misused intelligence bureau attracts and creates lazy and incompetent officers.

The taxpayer needs to be informed so that he can know what to expect and how well his public employees, the police, are doing their jobs. He will also be more knowledgeable about possible violations of civil rights, which intelligence-gathering may appear to violate. Questions regarding civil rights are especially important to the taxpayer because he pays either way. If police officers violate someone's civil rights, those rights might just be his. If they violate the rights of someone else and a lawsuit follows, the taxpayer pays the costs.

We're going to approach this topic in a way that's different from many handbooks. Instead of starting with organization and personnel, we're first going to consider the tasks a police intelligence bureau must undertake. Once we've got the responsibilities clearly laid out, we can consider the methods and the personnel that will carry them out. Finally, we will look at the organization necessary to support such an effort.

Introduction

The term *intelligence* dates back to the fourteenth century, when it was a synonym for information. Its use has since led to many misapprehensions. To police and civilians alike, intelligence is a much misunderstood concept. Some think of it as a military weapon, while others see it as the clandestine building-up of dossiers on unsavory characters and, often, political enemies. Some expect miracles from intelligence, while others feel that it is a tool of totalitarianism.

Gathering information is the heart of intelligence work. It is as vital for police as it is for the military, for statesmen, and for businessmen. It's not necessarily illicit, although it often appears to be so.

A vital point regarding intelligence is that it is useless if it remains inside the intelligence-gathering organization. Any intelligence bureau, be it military, political, or police, must pass the information on to its clients, the operational branches, to complete its job. We'll be discussing this point repeatedly in this book because this is often the weakest link in the intelligence chain. Sharing information is important both for completing a specific mission and generally to promote interdepartmental cooperation.

Readers will find that this book hits hard at the theme of interagency cooperation on several levels. The fragmentation of American policing has given criminals tremendous opportunities to pursue their activities undetected and/or unpunished. Not only do we have fifty states, each with its own penal code, but within those states we have a plethora of law-enforcement agencies, each going its own way. The relationship between them tends to be one of rivalry instead of cooperation. In each state, the state police or department of public safety is "El Supremo," and it sometimes treats county and local officers like poor relations. Federal agents, in turn, often act as if state and local officials are incompetent.

As we all know, police officers don't write the laws. They can't do much about getting a uniform penal code; instead, they will have to resign themselves to the fact that different states treat a specific crime differently. The punishment may be more severe in one state and less in another, while the same "illegal" act may be totally legal elsewhere. What police officers *can* do is foster interagency cooperation to enforce the laws as they are written.

Police intelligence officers have unusual latitude to do this. Intelligence-gathering depends less on statute than do many other aspects of police work. Intelligence officers are few, and they share a professional specialty, as do explosives technicians and examiners of questioned documents. This fact provides an opportunity for much more than merely sharing professional knowledge and information. In this book, we will see how intelligence officers can multiply their effectiveness by active exchange and pooling other resources.

Let's begin our examination with an historical look, because that will provide a background on which we can build. Modern police intelligence organizations are loosely based on military antecedents; because the police and military forces have different priorities, however, this has led to poorly organized and fragmented police intelligence bureaus in the past. In examining these factors, we can learn from the mistakes of the past.

Chapter 1
An Historical Look

During the nineteenth century, the intelligence function was limited to record keeping. In one sense, most detectives ran their own individual intelligence operations by cultivating informers, while undercover operators performed espionage, a form of intelligence-gathering. There was, however, no centralized intelligence function in most police departments around the country.

The larger police agencies, such as the New York City Police Department, maintained "rogues' galleries" for the information of their own detectives. These consisted of photographs, Bertillon measurements (a criminal identification system based on the clustering of certain physical traits), rap sheets, and other facts regarding specific criminals. The criminal population of the city was at the time small enough so that many detectives could keep most of the information in their heads. The morning lineup at police headquarters was for the benefit of detectives from all precincts who would then have the opportunity to observe the latest crop of arrestees.

Across the ocean, Scotland Yard established the Irish Special Branch in 1883, an early political and counter-espionage police force.[1] The functions of the Special Branch were to gather information about the Irish radicals of the era and to engage in law enforcement. Very shortly thereafter, the Special Branch expanded its surveillance to include anarchists and other politically extreme groups. However, in 1884, the Fenians, as the Irish Freedom Fighters were called, blew up the Special Branch offices. The Special Branch had its offices directly above a public urinal in Great Scotland Yard, a public square in London. Although there was a policeman on duty in front of the building at the time, the Fenians smuggled in a bomb and hid it in the urinal. It detonated on the evening of May 30, 1884, to the embarrassment of Scotland Yard officials.

Until the 1950s, there were no intelligence units as such in most police departments in the United States. The Los Angeles Police Department and a few other large agencies formed intelligence units, but these were primitive. The New York City Police Department, in a departure from relying only on the Bureau of Special Services and Investigations (BOSSI), formed the Criminal Intelligence Bureau, or CIB as it was then called. This organization underwent several name changes, possibly reflecting the confusion over its standing and duties. One of its founders was a "3x5 cards man," who put criminal information down on three-by-five-inch file cards during his thirty-year career. His card file formed the basis for the bureau's records, which were expanded and updated by other members.

It was not until the 1960s that a widespread recognition

of the need for an intelligence bureau within each police department arose. With the insight that organized crime was a national, and not merely local problem, the need for extensive exchanges of information became obvious. The widespread infiltration of organized crime into certain local agencies led to the formation of the Law Enforcement Intelligence Unit (LEIU), a private association of police officers that kept and exchanged information among members concerning organized crime.

Membership was limited to individuals (not agencies), who were selected by personal recommendation from other members who knew that the applicants were "clean." Meanwhile, even smaller agencies across the country were setting up intelligence units of sorts, with varying degrees of success.

There's a certain degree of keeping up with the Joneses in police work. Every several years, a new idea takes hold, and departments scramble to keep up with the latest fad. One such idea was the SWAT (Special Weapons and Tactics) team. Even tiny police agencies, unlikely to encounter terrorists or other serious threats, formed SWAT teams. These teams varied in competence because most small agencies lacked the time to train their members properly. This is also true with intelligence officers. Police administrators appointed intelligence officers without sufficient regard as to the need for the officers or their qualifications.

Chapter 2
What Intelligence Really Is

Intelligence has come to denote a type of information-gathering and use. It is special information used in carrying out policy or specific investigations. Intelligence actually consists of three parts or functions: collection, evaluation, and dissemination.

Collection

Information collected may be immediately relevant to a criminal investigation or it may become useful at a later date. The value of intelligence can be very far-reaching; it can confirm or supplement other information, or substantiate the value of an informant or other sources of information.

Related to information collection is the issue of information storage. This can be manual, as in a filing system, or electronic, as in a computer data base. In fact, each system has its place in police operations, and most police intelligence bureaus will need a hybrid system that includes both.

Evaluation

A simple and straightforward concept in principle, evaluation gets complicated when put into practice. The basic question confronting police officers in many investigations is whether or not the information is good. In police intelligence functions, evaluation will be on several levels. There will have to be an evaluation as to whether or not the information is likely or probable, based on its internal logic and its relation to other known facts.

There must also be an evaluation of the source. An informer may be venal, inventing "facts" for money, or the source can be mistaken. The source can also be well informed by being well placed for access to the information passed.

Dissemination

Getting information to the people who can use it is crucial. Without dissemination, any intelligence organization is only spinning its wheels. This is, however, where most such organizations fail miserably. Excessive secrecy can deprive potential clients of information needed to do their jobs. The passion for secrecy often overrides the need to know.

In setting up a plan for information dissemination, it is necessary to create categories of information so that sensitive intelligence sources will remain secret while noncritical information will be available to the largest possible number of police officers.

Chapter 3

What an Intelligence Unit Can Do

Many police officers, including senior administrators, have only a vague idea of a police intelligence unit's value. They don't understand the need for one or what it can do for the department.

The police are effective in different ways in different areas. Only in public-order functions, such as traffic control, can they meet a problem head-on and control it. Traffic police concentrate at choke points, direct traffic, and deal with violators.

In the fight against crime, the police are mainly a re-active force, coming on the scene after a crime has occurred in order to take a report and begin an investigation. They always appear to be a step behind the criminal. Intelligence, on the other hand, is "pro-active" police work. It's an effort to get a head start on the problem, instead of being forced into a passive and reactive role. The routine analysis and interpretation of information collected by the intelligence unit can help criminal investigators directly.

Immediate Investigations

The intelligence unit can save many crucial hours in the early stages of an investigation by providing "packages" of commonly available and routinely gathered information, such as a suspect's address, occupation, friends, and associates, and other documentary information, such as bank accounts and real estate and stock holdings. Information regarding driver's license and automobile registration is also part of the package. Such data can provide investigative leads. A department with Computer-Assisted Dispatch (CAD) needs many routine details to feed into its computer. This information tells an officer responding to a call whether there have been previous calls at the same address or that have involved the same people. Depending on the program, it can provide a great amount and variety of information to help the officer assess the situation before coming onto the scene.

Long-Range Information Packages

A well-organized intelligence unit can even provide information outside its immediate jurisdiction to help in long-range projects in its own department as well as others. All of this information can help with an investigation, but it takes time to assemble. Having it prepackaged and updated regularly can be an important time-saver.

Detailed Studies

Intelligence is more than the dry collection of offenses, arrests, and convictions listed on the typical yellow sheet or rap sheet. It is a detailed history of the criminal, his friends and associates, the organizations to which he belonged, and his accomplishments outside the criminal sphere. A criminal sometimes has talents that would not be listed on a rap sheet but that would be useful to an illegal enterprise. The intelligence unit keeps track of this sort of information and passes it on to those who can use it. A listing of a suspect's current associates can often give an indication as to his immediate future plans. If the subject in question is particularly important, such as an organized crime leader, a listing of his hangouts, habits, and schedules forms part of his intelligence file.

Other types of information helpful in long-term projects are a suspect's business holdings and associates. While it's not illegal to own a pizza shop or a Laundromat, for example, these holdings may be merely vehicles for laundering illegally earned income. If so, they may be subject to confiscation under the Racketeer Influenced or Corrupt Organizations (RICO) laws.

Predicting Crime Trends

Experience has shown that criminals are often one or more steps ahead of the law. They create and exploit opportunities for illicit profit and, when the criminal justice system reacts, they move on to other fields.

If properly run, an intelligence unit can identify and predict crime trends. It can also identify real and potential criminals. It doesn't take much imagination to predict that a new residential development or industrial park provides increased opportunities for burglars. Also, a certain type of business will attract a certain type of criminal. This is especially true with high-tech crimes.

Computer-related crime was predictable, given the increasing use of computers, but few intelligence officers foresaw that computer crime would become an extremely profitable enterprise that is very hard to detect and prosecute. The nature of computer crime made it all but inevitable that the majority of criminals would be insiders because the level of skill required precluded attacks by run-of-the-mill street criminals.

Another potential long-term trend deals with illicit traffic in human body parts. With the development of transplant technology, it doesn't take much imagination to foresee illicit transplants using bootleg body parts. Wealthy patients would pay large sums for new hearts or kidneys, and the lure of money would tempt some in the medical field to take some shortcuts to provide the needed organs.

At the lowest level, forging signatures on permission slips relating to young and healthy people killed in accidents would provide needed organs for those willing to risk discovery. A slightly more extreme step is for an emergency room doctor to tell relatives that the patient cannot survive, and to request permission to take needed organs. With permission, the surgeon would then ensure that the patient did not survive in order that he might strip the body.

Certain types of patients have always been victims of illicit medical experimentation whereby new treatments and drugs are tested without informed consent. The indigent, illiterate, and mentally retarded or defective have been compliant guinea pigs because they are usually in no position to protest and their relatives have either abandoned them or are untraceable. Without the danger of awkward questions from relatives, unethical doctors have been free to do what they wish with such patients.

If it is now possible to use people as unwitting guinea pigs and human blood banks, it would also be possible to use them as living organ banks. While it might be difficult to set up such an illicit project in a large hospital because someone may blow the whistle, a small hospital or clinic would be ideal for such an operation. The criteria for patient selection would be good physical health and a lack of relatives to visit and make inquiries. With these two conditions, it wouldn't be difficult to manufacture a medical chart indicating the presence of a fatal disease, and to have the patient succumb after a few days. The date on the death certificate would be the day that the final anesthetic was administered to permit removal of needed vital organs.

The final step in the development of a criminal enterprise dealing with organs would be to kidnap young and healthy people for vital body parts. A criminal gang would kidnap to order, much like a sophisticated vehicle-theft ring. Potential targets could be individuals such as runaway teenagers because they'd be unknown in their present locale and would have already been presumed reported as missing. This would minimize the risk of a police alert in the area.

This outline, based on publicly available information, makes it possible to sketch both warning signs and a profile of possible suspects. The discovery of a surgically mutilated corpse, with one or more organs neatly removed, would suggest an illicit organ ring, rather than "satanism," which many might normally deduce. Another sign would be repeated incongruities between police reports of injuries sustained during accidents and fatalities in emergency rooms. If slightly injured victims seemed more likely to die at a particular emergency room, this would justify a discreet investigation. If this emergency facility regularly supplied body parts for transplants, such an occurrence would be more than coincidence. Street informers might also report patterns in teenage disappearances. If a pattern emerged, such as several of them having responded to help-wanted ads or other possible lures, this might also furnish a lead for further investigation.

The high level of skill required in such an operation would dictate that medical personnel be involved. This isn't the type of crime that janitors and grave robbers could carry out. Tracing potential suspects would be remarkably easy, requiring only the interviewing of transplant surgeons regarding the origins of the body parts they worked with. If some such doctors came from small clinics and hospitals, which as we've seen would furnish discreet surroundings for illicit removals, this would be an important investigative lead for the intelligence unit.

Thus we see that a systematic analysis can predict a possible crime trend, even one based on advanced technology. An analysis can also provide several methods to detect such a trend before it becomes very advanced, as well as detecting a method of attacking the problem if it comes to the surface. A police intelligence unit, staffed by experienced and competent investigators, can routinely provide early warnings of crime trends.

Chapter 4

Collecting and Developing Information Sources

There are many types of intelligence collection, ranging from personal sources of information to very impersonal ones, including computerized and public records. Also included are: offense reports, witness statements, field interrogation cards, "Silent Witness" programs, parole reports, confessions, outside intelligence reports, informers, informants, undercover officers, physical and electronic surveillance, and public records.

Managing Information Collection

Collection, akin to spreading a net and gathering whatever comes in, often brings criticism from civil libertarians because of the variety of information collected. Collection is often indiscriminate, and can appear to be a "fishing expedition." Frankly, it often is. There is no way to prejudge or limit many intelligence operations. By definition, it's often impossible to know in advance exactly what information will come to the surface. It's also impossible to foresee how information will link up with information developed by other sources to produce a meaningful result. A wiretap of a gambling operation may also reveal a telephone call regarding drug traffic. The name of a person sought in one investigation may turn up in an intelligence operation covering a totally different area.

The intelligence officer must understand the concept of collateral information. This is information that can turn up unexpectedly during an investigation or as an adjunct to a separate effort. Collateral information acts as a multiplier, enabling more effective use of time and effort. While the average criminal investigator must keep his efforts narrowly focused to satisfy legal requirements for prosecution, the intelligence officer must do the opposite. He needs to gather as much information as he can from each possible source.

Courts frown on fishing expeditions. In filing an affidavit for a search or electronic eavesdropping warrant, police must specify the nature of the investigation and lay out the items they expect to find in the search. The court will exclude anything else. The purpose of this is to prevent abuses of warrants by police.

However, the court can't prevent a suspect from saying what he wishes over a telephone, freedom of speech being his constitutional right. If the information happens to touch upon another matter of interest to the police, that information is the concern of the intelligence officer because the criminal investigator can't use it under that warrant.

This is why it's bad policy to be very selective in gathering data. The intelligence officer should have an open-minded attitude and earnestly mine his sources for all the information they can provide. This requires careful categorizing, filing, and cross-referencing in order to preserve the information for use by those who need to know such information.

Information can be solid evidence, or frivolous and farfetched denunciations by malicious or flighty people. There's often no way to immediately check out a piece of information or a source's reliability. Experienced police officers know that it's unwise to accept information from many sources at face value and without corroboration. This policy makes it necessary to record the information for later evaluation, a policy that can lead to trouble if any of the information leaks out. Even the knowledge that a police intelligence bureau is collecting such information can cause no end of protests by those who don't understand the nature of intelligence.

An example of what can happen when knowledge of such information collection leaks out appeared on the front page of the *Arizona Republic* on July 7, 1988. The headline read: "Suspected AIDS Carriers Named in Sheriff, Police Files." The article stated that a citizen had seen the display on a police mobile data terminal that had him listed as a "High Risk: AIDS" case, although he stated that he'd never been tested for AIDS. The quality of the information was doubtful because the police had made the entry based on the fact that the man attended a party in a park with a group of men, some of whom were allegedly homosexual. The more important point, however, is that such information could do a lot of harm if carelessly disseminated.

As one can see, the tightest security is essential. The intelligence bureau should be housed away from police headquarters for maximum security. Security also involves keeping a very low profile. It's not enough to have a strong door with electronic locks and a sign that announces, *Warning! Authorized Personnel Only.* This sort of "security" attracts immediate attention. Sooner or later, the rumor mill informs everyone that the "spooks" are working behind the locked door.

It is possible for an alert and innovative intelligence officer to exploit existing information sources and often create new ones to aid in current or future investigations. In many cases, the information is available, but police officers don't take the extra step to obtain it.

Offense Reports

Anyone who has ever written reports must have sometimes wondered whether anyone ever reads them. Some reports receive inadequate follow-up, while others receive intensive investigation. A copy of each offense report should go to the intelligence officer (or bureau) because it might tie in with one of his projects. At least, it can serve as the groundwork for a later investigation or project. With computerized filing, retrieving the information is much easier and less laborious than before, and it is possible to store more information conveniently.

Witness Statements

Many witness statements are only of routine interest, but in certain cases an interview by the intelligence officer is worthwhile due to the nature of the investigation. If drugs or organized crime are involved, there may be more information available from a witness than elicited by the original investigating officer. The original interview is usually aimed only at obtaining information affecting the immediate investigation, not as data with long-range ramifications.

Field Interrogation Cards

The number of field interrogation (FI) cards varies greatly with individual departments. In many agencies, patrol officers spend so much time on calls that there is little time left for observing and stopping suspicious persons. In others, especially when officers fill in slow periods with self-initiated business, there may be many field interrogation cards.

Because of the glut of information, a necessary first step is to enter data from FI cards into the computer data base, thereby making it readily available when needed for a specific investigation or general search.

Another follow-up step is for the intelligence officer to scan the list of names, culling any of special interest, and interview the officer who filled out the FI card before his memory fades. Because the FI card allows only a very brief listing of the subject's characteristics and surroundings, there's always more to tell. Some of this information may be helpful in a long-range investigation.

Denunciations

Spontaneous denunciations by a criminal's friends, associates, rivals, and enemies sometimes help break a case or start a new one. This is especially true with drug deals, where a dealer finds it convenient to have the police eliminate his rival. This can result in a face-to-face meeting, but more likely only a letter or a phone call is needed.

Letters

Anonymous letters containing information regarding a crime are sometimes received by the police. Sometimes the information is specific enough to be very useful. At other times, it's too general to lead to a prosecution. Nevertheless, it should be ironclad policy to follow up on every such letter. Following up means interviewing the author, if identifiable. Otherwise, the files should be checked for similar letters and handwriting. The final disposition is to classify and file the letter for possible future retrieval.

Classification should be done according to several headings, such as:

1. Subject: drugs, murder, sex crimes, counterfeiting, etc.
2. Name of person denounced.
3. Place names and other identifying names, such as company names, contained in letter.
4. Date of letter.
5. Type of letter: handwritten, typed, postcard, etc.
6. Peculiarities unique to that letter, such as nickname, unusual paper or ink, etc.

These categories, although broad, will help to narrow down the search if subsequent letters on the same subject arrive. It's important to work out a brief code to enable you to enter the data into the computer for quick referral. Searching electronically is much quicker than poring through a manual filing system, as we shall soon see.

Silent Witness

Developing a silent witness program, with a toll-free number, can stimulate one type of intelligence-gathering. It can bring information from both suspects and citizens. If there is money in the budget to support it, a system of rewards for information leading to prosecution is workable. It's wise to keep the schedule of rewards small in order to avoid tempting those who might consider fabricating information.

Managing a silent witness program requires both firmness and tact. It is easier to run such programs today since they are well established and have credibility on the street.

A difficult problem that arises is maintaining the anonymity of the witness if so desired. Keeping the identity secret obviously precludes a face-to-face meeting, and makes the mode of payment more elaborate. The witness will demand cash and will probably specify the time and place of delivery. The officer making the drop should adhere strictly to the instructions and not try to discover the identity of the witness in order to avoid compromising future prospects. A silent witness program that burns people who contact it won't last long once the word spreads.

Searches

A search warrant literally provides the officer with an open door, and is consequently strictly controlled by the courts. This tight control is also why the intelligence officer must exploit the opportunity for a search warrant whenever it arises.

Ideally, an intelligence officer accompanies every search party serving a warrant. Practically speaking, there aren't enough hours in a day for intelligence officers to do this in most departments. This is one compelling reason to foster close cooperation between the intelligence bureau and the various arms of the criminal investigation division. Criminal investigators serving search warrants should keep alert to items that may not be covered by the warrant, but that would be of interest to the intelligence bureau.

The light weight and low price of photocopying machines can help in this effort. Officers executing search warrants should have one available in case documents are uncovered that might have intelligence value. It's quick and easy to set up a copy machine on a table, plug it in, and copy everything that might be relevant. Officers should always remember that, although what they copy may not be admissible as evidence, it may provide valuable investigative leads. Some of the more important considerations are:

1. Telephone directories. It's worth inspecting each one that is found, and opening it to any well-thumbed pages. There may be numbers underlined, and these may be significant. They may also be irrelevant, but the intelligence officer will be interested if the listing for Joe's Meat Market turns up underlined in directories inspected in several raids. Joe's Meat Market might in actuality be an illegal gambling establishment or a phone drop for a drug dealer.

2. Personal address books. If the warrant doesn't mention seizing these as evidence, it's vital to copy the pages.

3. Any lists of any sort. They may be "john" lists (those listing customers of a massage parlor or escort service) or appear to be shopping lists when in actuality they are code for something else. The intelligence officer should have an opportunity to evaluate these. Client lists for apparently legitimate businesses can also provide investigative leads. A dealer in stolen goods has clients to whom he sells such merchandise, and tracking them down might enable recovery of more stolen goods.

4. Officers should record a description and serial number of every appliance, vehicle, firearm, or other such valuable item on the premises. One

or more of these possessions might turn up on a list of stolen property. With computerized data processing, the likelihood of this happening increases every day.

5. Officers should also be alert to any stock, or commercial quantities of any goods or material, on the premises. A dozen video cassettes with the same title, for example, is stock, as would be a crate of scissors. Such quantities hint at stolen goods if the goods are not covered by invoices. In the case of the video cassettes, there might be a tape-pirating operation on the premises. Other stock might indicate the result of a "bust-out" operation conducted by organized crime.

6. Invoices of any sort are worth copying. Various types of criminal enterprises obtain their supplies from apparently legitimate businesses but may also be supplying criminal enterprises in the area. This makes their invoices investigative leads. An auto body repair shop may have invoices from wrecking yards that might be "chop shops," and invoices can be shortcuts to locating them.

7. Investigators who obtain search warrants should advise the intelligence officer if they expect much material to turn up, and give him the choice of accompanying them if he's free. They should understand that, rather than being a fifth wheel in the search, the intelligence officer may uncover information that will aid several other investigations.

Prison and Parole Reports

It is important to develop good relations with both prison officials and probation and parole officers. These sources can help build a profile of a subject, one that can provide leads in future investigations.

Prison reports can provide the following information, all of which should be recorded:

1. Medical records. These can be very important if it becomes necessary to verify an identity or to identify an unknown corpse.
2. Offense for which imprisoned.
3. Conduct during term of imprisonment, including tendencies toward violence and other deviant behavior. This can include records of infractions of rules regarding contraband and any behavior that provoked disciplinary measures. In evaluating this record, it's important to get an opinion from a prison official regarding whether or not the subject's behavior was within the normal range. Prisons are emotional pressure cookers and the inmates often violate rules that result in "paper," but that aren't very important. The level of violence in many prisons is very high, and becoming involved in an altercation may simply be normal behavior in that context.
4. Cell mates and other observed associates in prison. It is important to know who these people are because if it becomes possible to recruit a subject as an informer, it's helpful to have an outline of the persons about whom he can provide information.

5. Records of any interviews during the subject's prison term.
6. Records of visitors.
7. Names and addresses culled from both incoming and outgoing mail. This requires diligent record keeping, and many prisons don't bother to keep such extensive records.

Parole and probation officers can provide much more current information than prison reports, which will often be more valuable. It will include:

1. Current address and workplace.
2. Names and addresses of family members.
3. Names of current associates. This can provide leads to information obtainable if the subject becomes an informer.
4. Results of surprise inspections. This includes results of urine and blood tests, if administered.
5. Parole officer's estimate of subject's attitude and the likelihood of the subject's becoming involved in criminal activity after release.

Outside Intelligence Reports

Worth their weight in gold, outside intelligence reports are very hard to obtain because of the fragmentation of American police and the tendency of police officers to guard their information jealously. Obtaining reports from another agency's intelligence officer requires building a relationship of mutual trust. It can start by offering another officer information and hoping that sooner or later he will reciprocate.

The most one can expect from such a relationship is digested or processed information. It's too much to expect raw reports because these might reveal the source of the information. This can happen anyway if the material is documentary evidence taken during the service of a search warrant. It doesn't hurt the agency to provide photocopies of seized documents. However, if the source is a wiretap or bug, releasing a direct transcript would reveal the source; such is also the case with informers. It's necessary to accept the other intelligence officer's evaluation regarding the source's reliability.

Confessions

Handling a confession is similar to managing an informer. The intelligence officer won't usually be involved in a confession, but if there's good liaison between the criminal investigators and the intelligence bureau, investigators can alert the intelligence officer when something worthwhile comes along.

While information directly aiding the investigation at hand is the immediate concern of the investigator in charge of a particular case, the intelligence officer may want to obtain such collateral information as tips regarding sources of contraband, other criminal activities, receivers of stolen goods, and personal information regarding the subjects of special interest or other investigations.

Public Records

Public records can often disclose important information without requiring extensive research. Plat maps, county property tax records, and public-utility records reveal property owners and/or tenants. This can be very important when tracing hidden ownership while conducting organized crime investigations. The state motor-vehicle bureau is another agency that police officers consult daily. Making good use of public records is often a vital preliminary step in an investigation.

Exploiting Information Sources

Good source management involves extracting the greatest possible amount of information from each source. This means overcoming certain practical and legal obstacles, but the results often justify the effort. Whatever the source, it's important to milk it dry.

At the outset, the investigator must make himself aware of the prospects. A source may hold valuable information that is not related to a current investigation, but that would be worth tapping for future use. A source may also be able to provide information that will help another law-enforcement agency, and this is also worth exploiting.

The source may be a personal or impersonal one. An electronic monitoring device is a typical impersonal source that may disclose valuable information. Legislation and court rulings vary from year to year, and it may be illegal to record information not connected with a particular investigation, depending on the jurisdiction and the terms of the warrant. Nevertheless, the alert officer can take notes for informal use, thereby making effective use of his time, since the same monitoring device may be useful for several investigations. Granted, such information may be "tainted" and inadmissible as evidence. Investigators know that inadmissible information can often lead to other admissible evidence, requiring only proper exploitation.

Protecting a Source

It's vital to protect a source, even if the cost is the failure of an investigation. There are two very important reasons for this:

1. The source may be able to provide information useful to several investigations besides the current one.
2. ''Blowing'' a source is usually hazardous to his health and to the prospects of developing other sources. Potential snitches who feel that they will be betrayed by the police will keep their mouths shut.

When a body turns up in the trunk of a car, and the word goes out on the street that this was a snitch who got what he deserved, only two unpleasant conclusions are possible: the police failed to protect the source due to incompetence, or the criminal overlords have their own sources inside the police agency. The second possibility has happened often enough for the intelligence officer to take it seriously.

A source can be an impersonal one, but it too can be equally endangered. A wiretap or listening device can bring in vital information if it runs without interference. Once a target suspects that his conversations are being overheard, he'll be much more circumspect and may even have his home and business electronically debugged.

Ethics

The intelligence officer will face several ethical questions while managing his information sources. In many cases, these are covered by departmental policy. Some, however, are not. More importantly, there are cases that are officially covered by departmental policies, but with a tacit understanding that the officer can do as he pleases to get results. The only restriction is that he not get caught violating policy.

The officer should keep any promises he makes, regardless of departmental policy. This is simply good tactics because it helps build and maintain his reputation for square dealing.

Immunity requires coordination with the prosecutor's office. Generally, it's good practice to grant immunity for a lesser crime in order to convict the perpetrator of a more serious one.

In many cases, the officer can grant immunity on the spot for minor and even major infractions. An example is the informer who lights a joint in the officer's presence while giving information on a major case. It's obvious that arresting the informer would impede the investigation. In other ways, the officer may become aware that the informer is violating the law. An example of such a case is when an informer is carrying a concealed weapon where it's illegal. If the informer lives in a dangerous neighborhood where residents regularly arm themselves for defense, it's pointless to make an issue of this. The officer can't play straight arrow and arrest his informer for carrying a concealed weapon. To do so would be poor judgment.

In certain instances, the officer becomes a collaborator in what might be an illegal act. A silent witness or other informer who demands payment in cash probably won't declare this income, thereby violating the Internal Revenue Code. The intelligence officer cannot compromise his mission by turning a record of payments over to the Internal Revenue Service, since doing so would quickly silence his sources.

Payment is often in cash. If the money comes from departmental funds, the officer may be required to obtain a receipt. At times, the payment may be in merchandise. It may be possible, and even necessary, to pay the informer with a car or other property. This merchandise can come from material impounded or confiscated during an investigation or forfeited under a RICO (Racketeer Influenced or Corrupt Organization) statute.

Some informers ask for drugs to support their habits. It is obviously illegal for a police officer to deal in drugs. It's also clear that in certain locales, intelligence officers and criminal investigators do trade drugs for information. Officers sometimes furnish drugs for personal use, but not for resale.

Most often, departmental policy frowns on fraternization, but there's often an allowable exception in working informers. If it's necessary to party with an informer, the reward justifies it. However, officers must draw the line at committing crimes with their informers.

Chapter 5
Informers

Many people, including police officers, use the terms *informant* and *informer* interchangeably. The words are not the same, however. An informant is someone who provides information, but as a witness or victim. An informer is a co-conspirator or criminal associate who provides information for money or to secure another advantage, such as a reduced sentence or immunity from prosecution.

There are at least three types of informers: the agent in place, the defector, and the *agent provocateur*. The more common type is the agent in place, or snitch, who informs secretly and does not relinquish his status in the criminal hierarchy. This situation is more dangerous for the informer than the status of defector, because the snitch is within reach of reprisals if his actions are discovered. The penalty for informing is usually great physical harm—or death.

The defector comes over to the side of the law and in-

forms openly, relinquishing his place or status in the underworld. The open informer burns his bridges behind him,
because he can never go back. He might turn to informing
to avoid a heavy sentence on a serious charge or because he
is motivated by revenge. He also might decide to defect
because he finds himself in an untenable position in the
criminal hierarchy, such as having lost a power struggle
within the mob or gang.

The defector often appears as a prosecution witness. In
this very open role, he is in danger from the defendants, and
it is important to provide him with protection until the trial
is over. The task often doesn't stop then, because the witness must remain available in case of an appeal or retrial.
There's also the prospect of milking him for more information, and a dead defector can't talk, after all. Finally, there's
the public-relations aspect. If a witness-defector dies vio-
lently because the police failed to protect him, his death
will send a very clear message to others who might have
been thinking of defecting. This is why criminal gangs
make intensive efforts to eliminate defectors.

The agent provocateur is an informer who also under-
takes special tasks for his control officer, such as helping to
plan a crime in such a way as to make it easier for the
police to effect an arrest or facilitate prosecution after the
arrest. Using an informer as an agent provocateur is a very
valuable technique, because legal and practical difficulties
may make it impractical to use an undercover police officer.[1] Courts have repeatedly held that police officers may
not participate in crimes. Using an informer to fill this role
is a way of getting around such a problem.

Informers are sacred sources, but not because they're
necessarily splendid people. On the contrary, many confidential sources and snitches are what most police officers

would categorize as "scum bags." Their value is only in the information they can provide. In many instances, such sources are unreliable, venal, or totally untrustworthy, which is why criminal investigators tend to approach informers with caution, knowing that they're likely to be as immoral in their dealings with the police as in their dealings with their victims.

Developing an informer depends on both skill and luck. Skill in relating to people is important, for obvious reasons. Luck enters the picture when an officer encounters a potential informer at a vulnerable moment. The officer's skill and judgment then become important in developing the source. The personal relationship is all-important. At times, an act of simple kindness starts a relationship. In other cases, the officer works a twist, or coercion, on the subject to encourage cooperation. Sometimes, a mixture of the carrot and the stick encourages the best cooperation.

Managing the Relationship
A basic point to remember about handling an informer is that one officer should be the control, or contact, between the informer and the police agency, because it's possible to build a relationship between two individuals, but impossible to build one between an individual and an impersonal agency. The informer has a control officer to whom he provides information and from whom he obtains rewards. The control officer becomes familiar with the informer, his personality, needs, and moods, and can sense whether or not the relationship remains on the rails and whether the informer is playing square with him.

A trusting relationship with the informer is important. Trust, unfortunately, is often only one-sided. The subject must understand that the officer keeps his word; if the of-

ficer promises money, the officer must deliver. The officer
likewise should not promise the informer immunity from
prosecution unless he can deliver on such a promise. The
officer must make the informer understand that the officer
is reliable and predictable, even if the informer isn't. This
doesn't mean that the officer should play the role of sucker
for any deception the informer may attempt. On the contrary, the officer should make it clear to the subject that the
reward is strictly contingent on information received.

Intelligence officers can manage most informers on their
own, using only the resources of their office. In the case of
a witness-informer, there must be coordination with other
agencies, such as the prosecutor's office, since the resources needed to maintain such an informer can easily go
beyond what a local agency can provide. If the witness is
important enough to help on several levels, it may be worth
soliciting help from state and federal officials. In so doing,
the intelligence officer will have to guard against the
tendency of the higher agency, with its larger resources, to
move in and take over the case to the detriment of the local
agency's needs.

In the case of a witness-defector, there's an outright
mutual dependency relationship, with the advantage in the
officer's favor. If the informer doesn't deliver good information, the officer stands to lose an investigation, but if the
officer fails to protect his witness, the informer stands to
lose his life. The officer should never hesitate to exploit this
imbalance in the power relationship. Giving the informer
the impression that the officer will cut him loose by with-
drawing protection if he doesn't provide total cooperation
can often stimulate effort.

The power relationship can continue long after the trial
is over. If the defector has come over and is depending on a

promise of protection during the trial and relocation afterward, he'll continue to be dependent on the police officer. Relocation usually involves a change of identity, employment, and sustenance while seeking employment. This keeps the defector on the end of an umbilical cord that the officer can pinch off at any time. An officer who knows how to exploit this relationship can keep information coming long after a less-diligent or less-persistent officer would have concluded that his source had run dry.

The threat of cutting an informer loose during the initial stages can backfire if the informer calls the officer's bluff. A street-smart informer knows that a police officer is very reluctant to make good on such a threat because of the chilling effect doing so can have on his other snitches. A witness who gets killed after delivering himself to the care of a police officer will not be beneficial to that officer's reputation on the street. Once the prosecution is over and the relocation phase has begun, the officer can still exploit the informer. Cutting back on cash allowances or delaying payments are not final and irrevocable steps, and the officer can use these to keep his subject under control.

If there is strong interagency cooperation, an additional incentive to the informer can be subsistence payments from another agency's intelligence officer if the informer has something that would be of concern to him. While trading informers or allowing another investigator access to one's informers usually is out of the question, once a defector has revealed himself publicly, there is not as much to lose. If the informer has outlived his usefulness to the original intelligence investigator, giving a colleague in another agency the benefit of the informer's services builds goodwill between agencies. After all, the colleague may return the favor in the future.

Emotional Relationship

The emotional relationship between the officer and informer can become quite complicated. As a law officer, the investigator is an authority or father figure. Some aspects of the relationship can resemble a parent-child relationship:

1. The informer develops a dependency on the officer because the officer can provide money, food, or other sustenance the informer may not be able to provide for himself.
2. The informer may ask for, and receive, immunity from prosecution. This is very much like forgiveness from a parent.
3. The informer may start testing the investigator in order to explore how much he can manipulate or exploit the relationship. He may ask for things that the investigator may not be able to provide, such as immunity for future crimes and supplies of drugs. This is where the officer must firmly impose control by defining the limits of the relationship.
4. The informer can show signs of being eager to please the officer, which is good in that it fosters cooperation. The negative side to this is that the informer also may slant his information to conform to what he thinks the officer wants to hear. This is why the interrogator must be alert to the subtleties of the relationship and must diligently cross-check any information he receives from an informer.
5. The informer may ask the officer for advice regarding personal matters. If the relationship

reaches this point, it's a sign that the rapport is fairly solid.

One warning sign to look for is when the informer asks for advice much earlier in the relationship than the situation apparently justifies. It's important for the investigator to understand that informers, like other criminals, are not necessarily stupid and that they develop manipulative skills that are finely tuned. One such skill is to subtly flatter those whom they want to manipulate.

Managing an informer can take a great deal of patience and skill. The officer must understand from the start that it's definitely a manipulative relationship and that the informer will try to extract as much as he can from it. It's necessary for the control officer to understand the source and the motivations that influence him while keeping an emotional distance. It's also necessary to gather information for cross-checking every source. This is what leads to duplication, which to an outsider seems merely another example of inefficiency.

Informer Security

An informer who has defected presents only the normal bodyguarding problems. Those assigned to guard him should be well versed in bodyguarding techniques and understand that avoiding problems is a better strategy than coping with a confrontation. Accordingly, they should maintain a low profile and keep the defector out of sight.

The intelligence officer assigned as control to an informer must manage his communications so as not to compromise the informer. There are several purposes to meetings and communications: passing information one-way, debriefing or questioning, and payment. The most important are training and indoctrination, which help the informer survive long enough to become useful.

At the outset, the control officer must arrange times and places for meetings. He must instruct his informer as to how he should watch for a tail and how to get rid of any shadowers, as described in the chapter on security. The informer must memorize an emergency telephone number, at which he can leave a message any time, day or night, that will be quickly relayed to the control officer. The control officer should also instruct the informer in basic security techniques, such as never making an important telephone call from home or at work, where it would be easy to monitor the line.

A lot depends on the informer's intelligence and skill. Some are bright enough to understand immediately and to absorb the lessons thoroughly. They carry out their assignments with verve and skill and are almost a pleasure to have as informers. By contrast, others seem to be losers no matter what they try, and appear too dull even to memorize an emergency telephone number. They may even make the basic error of writing it down.

This is why the control officer must set up discreet contact procedures with fail-safe features to allow for unexpected problems. The emergency contact number should not be a regular police line. Anyone dialing that number should not hear "homicide" or "special services" at the other end. If a human operator answers, he or she should simply say the last four digits of the phone number, or simply "hello." An economical step is to have an answering machine on that line twenty-four hours a day. The telephone may be in the intelligence office, but nobody ever answers it when it rings. This prevents errors in answering procedure, or a caller's overhearing something from the office's background. The informer should either leave his message or, if he wants a call back, a number where the control officer can reach him immediately. The number should not be his home or work number.

Messages that aren't urgent may go to a mail drop. In the past, police officers have at times enlisted relatives to receive mail for them, but in certain types of investigations, this can be dangerous for anyone living at that address. A commercial mail drop is far more secure.

The address may nevertheless be compromised. This is why a mail drop with a lobby open twenty-four hours a day is preferable. Another type of mail drop operates by issuing clients a lobby key. The control officer should always check his box at a different time each day. This makes surveillance more difficult. The officer can spot surveillance if he arrives after normal business hours, when the street or parking lot is empty; anyone staking out the mail drop will be conspicuous.

The informer should watch for tails on the way to a meet, which, for obvious reasons, should be away from police headquarters. Another important point is that meets should never be at the intelligence office, even if the office is located discreetly away from other police facilities. The reason for this precaution is that allowing any informer into the office is a serious breach of security. He may redefect to the criminal side or reveal what he knows under duress. He may also take advantage of the opportunity to plant a bug, or listening device.

The officer should always arrange meets with different informers at different places. This is to safeguard an informer in case another is revealed. The actual sites are unimportant except that they should not be places where either person is known or frequents regularly. It is very indiscreet to be accosted or greeted by friends or acquaintances at a meet.

There are several desirable features a meeting place should have. It is helpful if it has several entrances. This allows arrival by one entrance and exit by another, an extra safeguard against surveillance. Another plus is the proximity to public transportation or a public parking lot for easy access.

There are several security procedures the control officer may find helpful when going to a meet. One is to bring a backup officer or team with him. An important security procedure is to meet the informer at the previously arranged place and immediately leave for another once contact is made with the informer. This allows the opportunity for the backup to check the informer for a tail.

Another suggestion is to select a meeting place with more than one approach route and to instruct the informer which route to use. The control officer can then observe the informer during his travel or even intercept him before he reaches the meet and then lead him elsewhere.

These security measures can be valuable if the control officer suspects duplicity from his informer; they also help to avoid an ambush. Heavy-duty dope wholesalers have shown that they don't hesitate to kill police officers, and if the investigation touches them, deadly attack is a constant danger to police officers (this is good reason for wearing body armor to a drug meet).

There are other steps an intelligence officer can take to help maintain his informer's security. One is to divert attention away from the informer by having meetings with several others in his circle of acquaintances. This can be by the use of quick field interrogations in the street or by visiting the acquaintances ostentatiously at home. If, by luck, one of them commits an offense and gets arrested, this offers a splendid opportunity to stage a diversion.

A more drastic step involves "framing" someone else as an informer. The technique involves pulling someone in for interrogation or arresting him on a real charge or a pretext. The officer then drives the person back to his usual haunt after a couple of hours. While dropping him off, the officer acts very friendly and shortly afterward he and other officers arrest or interrogate someone else in the group. This will generate suspicion against the person who was first picked up, helping to protect the actual informer.

Getting the Most from an Informer

Exploiting an informer for maximum information requires that he be questioned on several different levels. Military intelligence officers classify intelligence as strategic and tactical, separating the two with regard to the processing of captured enemy personnel. Upon capture, prisoners go to a quick interrogation center, where intelligence officers search them for documents and question them regarding their units and the situation immediately behind the front. The next step for the prisoner is the strategic interrogation camp, where intelligence officers attempt to find out more information through deeper questioning. Topics can include morale on the enemy home front, regularity of mail from home, quality of training, and other factors that bear upon long-range evaluations of enemy effectiveness.

Police intelligence officers, on the other hand, have to take an even wider view because their subjects often can provide more detailed information, some of which can be useful to other agencies. The police intelligence officer has to consider these wider needs in setting up his priorities.

Another purpose of a far-reaching line of questioning is the cross-checking of the subject's information. In some cases, the informer may not be in a position to know the information he claims to be disclosing, and gathering details helps to establish the validity of other information.

The usual set of priorities in questioning is as follows:

1. Information to help in the immediate investigation. The questioning may even be in response to a request by a criminal investigator for help in developing information bearing on a high-priority investigation.
2. Information bearing on other crimes within the jurisdiction. Passing this on to investigators can help them build a case.
3. Background information relating to crime and related personalities within the jurisdiction. This can be the street price of drugs and areas of influence of specific criminal organizations.
4. Information that can help other police agencies. An informer may have spent some time in another locale, and may have very valuable information about conditions there. While of no direct interest to the intelligence officer, such information can help his counterpart in the other agency.
5. Personal background information. This often overlaps with other categories, especially Category 4, and it can help to develop specific criminal information as well as verifying the accuracy of other information provided.

Questioning an informer thoroughly inevitably takes many sessions. The intelligence officer operates on the principle that he can take the informer's cooperation for granted. In this regard, the relationship isn't like a criminal interrogation. There are other problems, though, as outlined above. The informer may not know the information he claims to know, he may be fabricating or slanting his information to please his questioner, or he may be inventing information for financial reward. Overcoming these possible problems requires a knowledgeable officer and the careful elicitation of details from the informer. The details are important because they often allow verification of the informer's story, or they can show the interrogator where the story doesn't check out.

It's important to obtain an inventory of the subject's knowledge as soon as possible after meeting the immediate need, which can be accomplished as a result of a discussion covering the subject's life history. It's helpful to record details at this stage for comparison with later accounts. A life history provides the officer an outline of where the subject has been, what he has done, and—by inference—what he knows. Working with this information, the officer can develop a plan for systematically eliciting information.

A checklist for questioning should cover at least the following:

1. Present address and telephone number
2. Past addresses and telephone numbers
3. Present employment
4. Family and friends
5. Addresses and telephone numbers of persons mentioned
6. Criminal affiliations
7. Location of physical evidence

8. Informer's criminal record, including from other locales
9. Impressions of arresting officers
10. Knowledge of corrupt police officers
11. Other criminal personalities known
12. Background criminal information, including the availability of illegal drugs, persons engaged in trafficking, availability of illegal firearms, persons engaged in trafficking, and sources of illegal documents
13. Prison record, including terms served, where served, names of cell mates, names of other associates, status of prison gangs, availability of contraband, smuggling in prison, names of smugglers, names of guards smuggling, and prison underground economy

There should also be a narrative of the informer's history and lifestyle. This can disclose valuable details if the officer keeps alert. One area to cover is the time the informer spent as a fugitive, if he did so. How the subject supported himself and provided housing and transportation is worth knowing. This often touches upon illegal activities, such as stolen or forged ID and crimes committed for sustenance.

Checking out the information obtained from informers is necessary, and it can bring collateral benefits. Validating the information provides a guide as to how well the officer can trust the informer. In so doing, it's often necessary to check with other officers, who may appreciate the information. This is especially true when working with another agency. Approaching another agency's intelligence officer to request verification of certain allegations and offering to develop more information for their benefit if the informer turns out to be reliable is a good way of building a mutually helpful relationship between agencies.

Probably the greatest weakness among American police is fragmentation. There are many jurisdictions at various levels, and cooperation is often unsatisfactory. Instead, we see interagency rivalries that degrade the law-enforcement effort. A good way to build the necessary bridges is to exchange information.

The poor relations in the American criminal justice system are the corrections officers. Prison guards and administrators are poorly paid compared to police officers, and working conditions are worse. This accounts for a turnover rate that is higher than that among police officers. Another problem prison administrators face is that police agencies often tap them for information but rarely supply them with any. A police intelligence officer who contacts a prison administrator with information about problems within the prison, developed from interviewing informers, will make a friend and be able to solicit cooperation when he needs it.

The interrogating officer must listen to the informer on several levels. The first concern will usually be information of immediate interest to him and his agency. However, he should also listen for what may later turn out to be vital information, the significance of which the informer doesn't realize. A casual statement by an informer may be the first indication an intelligence officer receives of a new crime trend or a new facet of organized crime. Keeping alert to these possibilities can help reduce the lead that criminals often seem to have over the law.

1. Rapp, Burt. *Undercover Work* (Port Townsend, WA: Loompanics Unlimited, 1986), p. 111-114.

Chapter 6

Undercover Officers

There's a strong tendency to glamorize and romanticize undercover officers, often in complete disregard for their actual accomplishments. Having an undercover officer is often a status symbol among police departments, proof that the agency is large enough to afford or justify one.

In reality, however, undercover work is very labor-intensive. This is why it's necessary to balance the effort against possible rewards. In certain cases, having under-cover officers has been a waste of talent. Local police in a large university town maintained one, and sometimes two, undercover officers during the student protest days of the late 1960s and early 1970s. At the same time that burglary rings, vehicle theft rings, and chop shops were developing in the area, undercover officers were concentrating on finding out the time and place of the next demonstration, information that was available through other sources.

An undercover officer with a cost-effective assignment can help the intelligence effort. This is demanding and often unrewarding duty. The subject of an undercover effort may die, move away, go on vacation, or otherwise become unavailable. Other incidents can occur to impede an investigation. In certain situations, though, undercover work can develop information unavailable through other means.

Management

There is a good case to be made that the undercover officer should be under the control and management of the intelligence officers. The main fact is that undercover work is uncertain. The officer employed to aid a specific investigation may not be able to make contact with the subjects or penetrate a ring. He or she may also develop information useful in another field. If the undercover officer is under the control of a detective assigned to a specific investigation, the detective is unlikely to pay much attention to collateral information, perhaps ignoring it altogether. This is why effective management must be under the control of a person who can see the big picture.

The intelligence officer, aware of the needs of investigators in several different fields, can best determine the course of the undercover work. If the effort in one investigation becomes stalled, he can redirect it to another field.

Recruitment

Recruiting the undercover officer requires finding an officer who is not known on the street. This is why many intelligence officers recruit their undercover officers from police applicants. In some cases, it's wise to train the undercover officer secretly instead of sending him or her to the academy.

For undercover work, the training can be very abbreviated, especially because most of the topics normally covered in the academy will be useless. The undercover officer never makes traffic stops, and doesn't need to know the traffic code in all its ramifications. Likewise, most of the departmental paperwork will be foreign to him. He'll have to submit reports, but these can be in a simple narrative format; for this, the ability to write coherent sentences is all that is necessary. Most of the qualities the officer will need to carry out his undercover assignment are qualities people already have, not qualities they develop.

The recruiting officer will most likely also be his training officer. He'll have to explain the assignment in detail, covering the recent history of undercover efforts, if any, in that locale, and the results obtained. The new undercover officer will need to know what information the intelligence officer needs from him; for this the intelligence officer will have to compile a shopping list. He will have to develop his cover with the help of his training officer, and learn the arrangements for his pay and his contacts. He'll need to memorize the times and locations of meetings with his control officer, and learn methods of ensuring that he is not followed on the way to meetings. He'll also need to memorize a contact telephone number for emergencies. This is a number manned twenty-four hours a day, through which he can get an emergency message to his control officer.

Another part of his briefing will cover recognition. If there are other undercover officers in the area, he should meet them so that they will know each other and avoid the possibility of working at cross-purposes out in the field. There should also be a recognition signal in case of contact with patrol officers. This can prevent mistaken identifications and their potentially serious consequences.

The prospective undercover officer must be a good actor and be willing to put in much more than forty hours a week. He must also be willing to break off contact with his friends and family for weeks or months. He must be able to blend in with his target group, have emotional fortitude, be able to improvise and think on his feet, and have a good memory for names and faces. [1]

Cover

The undercover officer must have a cover, a plausible story regarding who he is, from where he came, what he does for a living, and other facets of his life. The cover need not be totally unbreakable, as it's unlikely that the undercover officer will encounter intensive investigation of the sort done on police recruits. As we'll see, there are simpler ways for criminals to check out people they meet.

Establishing cover may require that the officer set up a domicile to support the cover. This must be an address in an area where he's unknown so that he won't be likely to have his cover blown by meeting someone who calls him by his correct name.

There are no guarantees that the officer won't meet someone who will blow his cover. If he works an area he hasn't frequented before, he can still encounter someone who has moved from his old locale (criminals are mobile, too, after all). If the undercover officer claims to be a real person, he may encounter someone who knew that person elsewhere, such as in prison, and who will be able to reveal the deception. This is why the undercover officer must be prepared with a course of action if his cover is inadvertently blown.

"Backstopping" the cover may be necessary in some

cases. For example, the officer can provide a work history or other support for his fictitious past. Having a contact at a legitimate business in another city who will verify the undercover personality's employment is one way to back-stop. Providing the officer with documentation that will stand up to examination is important; a routine traffic stop can expose a forged driver's license the undercover officer may have in his possession, thereby possibly blowing his cover.

Infiltration

Infiltrating a criminal gang still won't be easy for the most skilled undercover officers. Often targets of under-cover operatives, criminals have become more sophisti-cated. Some have found close associates testifying against them at their trials and have passed warnings on to their successors.

Many organized crime families won't accept people they don't know or have only recently met, recruiting instead among relatives or long-term friends. Bikers and other gang member types involved in drug traffic are more transient, devising tests to screen their applicants. For example, they know that police officers are not allowed to commit crimes to support their cover. To weed out undercover officers, therefore, they insist that a potential member participate in a serious crime as a condition of admission to full mem-bership. In some cases, the crime is murder.

This is why it's almost impossible for an undercover officer to find full acceptance in a criminal gang. Instead, he has to work the fringes and hope to pick up what he can. In the world of drug trafficking, he can pose as a customer, finding a dealer and setting him up for a bust. However, working arrests is not the most effective way to employ an undercover officer because it's not cost-effective to recruit and train an officer for a few low-level busts. The cost of setting up effective cover demands more return on the investment.

In some cases, a superficial cover is enough. An officer unknown in the area can pose as a customer to take down a consumer fraud operation. An example of this is medical quackery, in which an officer can answer an advertisement and gather evidence while posing as a patient. Another example is the auto theft and chop-shop racket, in which an undercover officer can bring his vehicle to a body shop for repair. Forensic examination after the repair has been done can determine whether the body shop used stolen parts.

Cooperation Between Departments

Interagency cooperation should not be limited to exchanges of information. There's a lot to gain from exchanging undercover officers.

Undercover officers can be much more effective when swapped. The smaller the agency, the more likely its undercover officer will become blown after only a short while. When this happens, the officer is forced to return to patrol or another regular assignment. This can be a severe loss if the officer has genuine talent for undercover work.

Adjacent agencies can exchange undercover officers in order to maintain their freshness. An agreement to exchange officers to work the new territories can extend the useful lives of undercover officers. Although American policing is administratively fragmented, perceptive officers and administrators can encourage cooperation and thereby reduce the advantage enjoyed by criminal elements profiting from the lack of police coordination.

Mistaken Identity

A potentially serious problem that can arise is that a patrol officer can mistake an undercover operative for a felon. This happens when an outside state or federal agency operates an undercover officer in the area without telling the local agency. This often results when the higher agency experiences a feeling of elitism, but it can lead to an erroneous shooting in certain circumstances. If, for example, the undercover officer makes an arrest or holds a suspect at gunpoint, he should have his identification displayed when a marked unit arrives. The problem comes if the undercover officer isn't carrying ID. Another dangerous situation occurs when the officer is involved in a shoot-out with suspects. Responding officers won't be able to tell which are the suspects and which are the officers. This reiterates the importance of recognition signals. These can be code words or commonly used phrases. A traditional one in New York City is, "I'm on the job."

Integrating Undercover Work

Undercover officers should not operate in a vacuum. The undercover officer can develop new sources of information that confirms that provided by an informer. The intelligence officer can plan the assignments so that the undercover effort complements other intelligence sources. Such a process requires both good planning and imagination, and the potential rewards make the effort worthwhile.

1. Rapp, Burt. *Undercover Work* (Port Townsend, WA: Loompanics Unlimited, 1986), p. 34.

Chapter 7
Surveillance

Surveillance can be very labor-intensive or economical, depending on the type conducted and the locale. Physical surveillance consumes many man-hours and is justifiable only in critically important cases. Electronic surveillance is very cost-effective but is subject to legal limitations that may impede an investigation.

Physical Surveillance

Physical surveillance is comprised of stationary surveillance or moving surveillance. Stationary surveillance requires that an observation post be established from which arrivals, departures, and other events at a fixed place are observed. Moving surveillance, also known as shadowing or tailing, may be conducted on foot or with a vehicle.

STATIONARY SURVEILLANCE

An observation post itself can be stationary or mobile. Setting up a fixed observation post requires renting or buying premises from which it's possible to run the surveillance. At times, helpful citizens will allow officers to use their premises for this purpose. In this regard, officers allowed this privilege must maintain very good relations with the citizens in order to encourage future cooperation.

It's often best to have the observation post anywhere but directly opposite the premises under observation in order to avoid detection. A room with a window overlooking the suspect premises usually is adequate.

Any sort of vehicle can be used as a mobile observation post, but a van, truck, camper, or motor home is ideal. Having two men in a car is Hollywood police work; while it may work in a pinch, it becomes conspicuous in a long-term surveillance operation.

Officers setting up an observation post must prepare for long hours and intensive surveillance. They must not allow themselves to be seen when setting up the post and also must be discreet when changing shifts. This is why an entrance around the corner is desirable for an observation post located in a building. If officers are using a van or other vehicle, it must have living facilities suitable for several days of habitation. In setting up such a post, anyone on the street should see the vehicle drive up, and someone leave it. If the driver doesn't leave and lock the door after him, he will arouse suspicion. The officers inside are there for the duration. There's no going down to the corner to bring back a pizza, for example.

Two officers at one time are usually enough to do the job competently. In a pinch, one can do it, but he may have trouble staying awake. If audio surveillance is also being conducted, three or more officers might be necessary, with at least one assigned to man the headset.

The team should depend on optical aids to help reduce fatigue. While observing, they should also keep away from windows, careful not to produce reflections with optical instruments. There should be enough light inside the observation post so that a log can be kept, as well as a camera with a telephoto lens for photographing. It may not be desirable to risk showing a light at night. A small tape recorder will serve as well.

MOVING SURVEILLANCE

Moving surveillance is more labor-intensive than simple observation because it takes more officers to run a competent tail than to staff an observation post. The success of a moving surveillance operation depends on whether the subject is aware he is possibly being tailed and the steps he takes to check for a tail. If the subject is totally unaware that anyone might want to shadow him, one officer may be enough for the job. A suspicious or street-smart subject is more likely to check for tails. Shadowing such a subject requires more sophisticated methods and more officers. A larger team enables the close tail to be changed frequently or the replacement of any members whose covers might have been blown.

A vehicular tail requires several vehicles, ranging from passenger sedans to a pickup or van. It's easier to tail inconspicuously in urban areas than in rural ones. An electronic aid, such as a bumper beeper, can help keep track of a subject vehicle while the tailing vehicle remains out of sight.

In selecting the method to use, it's important to take into account the subject's skill and sophistication. There might be an unpleasant surprise down the road, such as his detecting the bumper beeper and placing it on another vehicle going in another direction. A foot team shadowing a subject in a city might find him going into a major train station so that he can blend into the crowd.

A foot team has to be prepared for the subject who starts down a deserted street and then breaks into a run. Another tactic he may use is to speed up and slow down, to see who is keeping pace with him. Some sophisticated subjects have a convoy, a confederate who tails them to detect whether anyone is following the subject. [1]

Electronic Surveillance

Electronic surveillance may be court-ordered or extracurricular. It's impossible to generalize about the requirements for a warrant, because laws vary so much from state to state and court decisions change from year to year. Suffice to say that if the law allows it, electronic surveillance with a court order is preferable.

A court order is absolutely essential if the investigator wants to use a transcript for evidence in court. For the intelligence officer, however, it's not as necessary, since he's seeking investigative leads or long-range information.

For our purposes, we will discuss here two types of electronic surveillance: telephone tapping and placing a bug inside the subject's premises.

TELEPHONE TAPS

The simplest and easiest way to arrange for a telephone tap is to contact the local telephone company's security officer and show him a copy of the court order. He will then arrange for a tap at the frame and a line to the intelligence office. This makes it extremely convenient.

Without a court order, it's necessary to find a place between the subject's telephone and the central office where the tap can be placed. The tap can be an induction pickup or a physical connection to his pair of lines. The induction pickup works well only if there's one pair, because it will pick up everything within its range and other lines will interfere with the desired pickup. A physical tap can be at the junction box, located in the basement of the building or on the street or alley in a residential block with one-family houses.

The preferable method to set up the tap is to place a small radio transmitter on the tap. There are two reasons for this: security and access. There must be no physical connection between the tap and the officer's listening post, because if the tap is illegal, it would compromise the officer. Regarding access, it might be very difficult to keep an officer at the junction box, especially one exposed to view, with a set of headphones. If there's a tape recorder attached, someone needs access to change the tape and batteries periodically.

BUGS

Bugs are also primarily of two basic types: wired and radio. The wired listening device is a microphone with wires leading to the listening post. This type is harder to install and harder to detect. The radio bug contains a microphone and small transmitter. It's only necessary to place it in the room and leave; because it transmits radio waves, however, it's very easy to detect in a casual sweep.

Gaining access to the premises may not be possible at all, if it is well guarded or otherwise secured. There are several methods that are very uncertain, such as posing as a telephone repairman or delivering a bouquet of flowers.

These methods belong in the pages of detective novels and rarely work in real life.

The professional methods are less risky. One is to send the target a gift with a bug placed inside. If the target is a book collector, a book would, of course, be ideal. This is where knowledge of the target and his habits and preferences is important. It might be possible to arrange with one of his suppliers to send a legitimate object with a listening device inside.

An informer who has access to the premises can place the bug. Another method to employ is surreptitious entry. This requires knowing when the subject will be away and what security measures are in effect in addition to the ability to get in and out without leaving a trace. This tactic, however, provides the opportunity to place a wired bug, which can be longer-lasting than one that uses batteries.

If there is solid information that the subject will be staying for a short time in premises that don't belong to him, such as a hotel room, it might be possible to get in ahead of him to place a bug. This offers more safety for the officer.

Battery life is a problem. There simply aren't any batteries that will power a transmitter for more than a few days, thereby limiting the usefulness of bugs. One expedient that works in some situations is to place a bug in a device that is plugged into the wall, such as a lamp or stereo set.

If the bug is the wired type, the wires must terminate in a transmitter in order to break any physical connection with the officer in case of discovery. A receiver must be within range to pick up the transmissions. With wireless bugs, of course, it's also necessary to have a manned or unmanned listening post within range. A tape recorder will service an unmanned post. The machine must be of the VOX (voice-activated) type, as a continually running tape is useful for only two hours at most. Using a tape recorder instead of a live listener can make a wiretap or bug very economical.

A manned listening post can also be utilized, which can be more useful if the investigation relates to a short-term project. Often, knowing the target's plans as they are unfolding can be helpful, and for this only a live listening post will do. Fortunately, these occasions don't occur very often.

A tape recorder is essential for several reasons. It provides a permanent record, as any one listener may not be able to take notes quickly enough to write down all that is said. Some people speak very quickly or have indistinct speech, so that several hearings are required in order to understand the material. With regard to telephone taps, the subject will be dialing numbers, and it's important to know whom he contacts. When only the pulse dialing system was in use, a very expensive machine known as a pen register was used, which would record on a paper graph the pulses of a dialed number. Today, with the touch-tone system, the pen register is inadequate. Only a tape recorder will record the tones of a number.

Some court decisions have held tape recorder and unmanned listening posts to be inadmissible because they record indiscriminately, capturing even innocent people on the tape. This can be crucial if the case is to go to trial and electronic evidence is part of the prosecution's case. For the intelligence officer simply seeking information to develop investigative leads, such considerations are not important.

1. Rapp, Burt. *Shadowing and Surveillance* (Port Townsend, WA: Loompanics Unlimited, 1986), p. 21-23.

Chapter 8
Storing Information

Today, more than ever, there's an information glut. There are so many names to record and so much information about each one that the task can be uncontrollable. In all but the smallest jurisdictions, there's so much information to process that no single person can keep track of it all. This is why information management is a critical task; without effective information management, any intelligence effort is bound to be degraded.

For many years, the classic method of storing information was the three-by-five-inch file card. It can still be of use in some agencies if there's not much information to store, but it quickly becomes cumbersome when there's a need to cross-reference information or retrieve it quickly. The physical bulk of the files becomes an obstacle when there are more than about ten thousand cards.

Raw information is just that: raw. It's not very useful

without processing. The first thing to do is to devise a system for information storage and retrieval, which can be manual or electronic. Most likely, it will be a hybrid form.

Why hybrid? One reason is cost; only the largest computer can store all of the information needed. Another reason is the variety of information needed in an intelligence file. There can be narratives, affidavits, newspaper accounts, photographs, and other forms of information that are impossible to store on any but the largest and most sophisticated computers. There are comprehensive systems for storing files, including fingerprints and photographs. Only the largest and most generously funded agencies have these types of computers.

The picture is changing, though. Several companies are working on medium-level systems that place complex computer information systems within the reach of medium-size agencies. With the new generation of computer chips and new programs to exploit them, the prices of sophisticated systems continue to drop.

These systems, some of which are still under development, are too new to evaluate accurately and are still out of the reach of many agencies. Therefore, the focus here will be on the smaller systems, which are obtainable by the smallest intelligence bureau.

Documents are still the mainstay of law-enforcement bureaucracy. Witnesses still sign paper statements, and the courts still expect paper affidavits, statements, confessions, and transcripts. A hybrid system can satisfy many needs.

Basic Concepts
The computer reduces the space needed for data storage and makes information retrieval easier, speeding up the entire process. A basic PC-type computer can use a data-

base program to index and cross-index a large number of paper files.

The tremendous advantage of electronic data processing is speed. If, for example, it becomes necessary to generate a list of ex-convicts within a certain geographical area who own automobiles, a printout can be ready in a couple of minutes. Likewise, it's possible to take a list of names in an investigation and run them through the computer to see what turns up.

The computer is only as good as the information that is fed into it. There is an expression, "GIGO," familiar to computer programmers and engineers, meaning, "Garbage In, Garbage Out." False information erroneously fed into a computer will cause problems down the road, as will the misinterpretation of information obtained from the computer files.

If an investigator requests a computer check on a list of names developed during an investigation, and one of the names shows a previous involvement in a similar investigation, it's important not to jump to a conclusion. This might mean that the person had indeed committed a crime at one time, but it also might be coincidental. A computer listing does not equal a conviction. As we saw in the AIDS case cited previously, raw information can be misleading. The information is an indication that additional investigation is needed, and the diligent investigator will check the paperwork to discover what the person's role was in the previous investigation. It will also help to interview the investigator in the earlier case in order to gain additional information if he remembers much about the case.

Selecting Hardware

It's vital to use a computer for intelligence information

that is separate from the main departmental computer. While there are some computers that can run several programs, using passwords to keep the confidentiality of a sensitive bank of information, all of these can be defeated. The compromise to security often comes accidentally, not by design, because one or more of the operators does something foolish, like writing the password on a slip of paper and leaving it in a desk drawer.

Always select a computer that has more memory than you might require initially, since information stored tends to grow out of proportion to the size of the intelligence unit, and there is always a need for more capacity. At the outset, you'll find that there is already a wealth of information available to down-load from the National Crime Information Center (NCIC) and state computers.

The usefulness of a computer data bank grows out of proportion to the information stored within it. The more information stored, the easier it becomes to establish correlations and links, the relationships between people, events, and organizations that often put an investigation on the right track.

In this section, we'll discuss in detail PC-type computers and their capabilities because the majority of police agencies in this country are small and are likely to have only PC-type machines. Larger machines come with very comprehensive manufacturer support, and the purchase price usually includes a training program for the users.

Security and Storage

Any damage to files, be they paper or electronic, can undo years of work. The chapter on security will cover how to safeguard files as well as other aspects of an intelligence operation. For the moment, let's lay out one main principle of safeguarding electronic data: *Back up all data*. This means making an electronic copy, be it on tape or disk, of everything worth saving. This is insurance against the chance that a disk or tape is erased accidentally or otherwise damaged.

Information Management

The basic tool of information management is a data-base program. This is simply an electronic filing system. Though it cannot totally replace a paper system, it speeds up access and handling of information immeasurably.

There are many data-base programs available for small computers. Some are individual programs, such as Dbase III, while others are part of an integrated system which also includes word processing and spreadsheets. The integrated system is designed for business use. A police agency would find it convenient to have one of these systems because it would provide an electronic office, which would be useful for composing letters, reports, and affidavits, calculating budgets, and normal criminal information functions. However, a police intelligence officer needs only the data base.

Obtaining only a data base is cheaper than an integrated system and saves memory space in the computer. Data-base programs range from a few dollars to many hundreds of dollars; each user will have to determine whether or not the extra bells and whistles on some programs are worthwhile in the long run.

All data bases have certain common features, and we'll run through the important ones here. This will show how to get the best use from a data base and provide a realistic idea of what is possible.

Entering Data

Using a data base is not merely a matter of punching in data and having the machine magically sort it out. It's necessary to decide what is worth storing and in which categories. Let's start with a concrete example, and assume that we're setting up a data base on persons who may be suspects, convicted felons, witnesses, or complainants. To make maximum use of the data base, we have to provide certain details about each name.

Each *record* stands for one person. Within each record, there are categories of information that we call *fields*. It's necessary to decide how many fields we want and how large each field will be. The basic principle to keep in mind is that the more information stored for each record, the fewer records we'll be able to handle within a limited memory.

In round numbers, if we list only the name, address, and telephone number for each person, we may be able to squeeze ten thousand records on one disk. If we want to list more information, we'll find our capacity cut down in proportion to the amount of information we include for each name.

Here are some fields we'll surely need:

> Last name
> First name and middle initial
> Street address
> City
> State
> ZIP code
> Telephone number
> Date of birth
> Social security number

These are the basic identifiers necessary for each person listed. Allocating the space each field takes up is the next decision. Both first and last names need about twenty spaces, as few names are longer than that. The street address should have twenty-five or thirty spaces, while the city usually takes fifteen or twenty. To save space, only two spaces will be used for the state. The telephone number takes twelve spaces, because it should include the area code and a space or hyphen separating each part of the number. The ZIP code may be only five spaces; with the four-digit supplements, however, it might be wise to allow a total of ten spaces. The date of birth needs eight spaces; the social security number takes eleven spaces.

These entries are just the basics. For intelligence purposes, it will be necessary to include several other fields. In designing them, it's important to keep in mind that coding can save space. For example, it's not necessary to allocate space to spell out "convicted felon." One space will do for this category, with "F" standing for felon, "W" for witness, "C" for complainant, "P" for psycho, and "S" for suspect.

It may be desirable to include a field for aliases. Another field could list organized crime connections, if any. It's also helpful to list occupation, nearest relative, driver's license number, type of vehicle owned, plate number, and other identifying details. A field could be reserved for the type of offense the person usually commits. A one-digit code would save space, as it's rarely necessary to be very specific for this purpose. One possible code listing would be:

1. Homicide
2. Assault, simple or aggravated
3. Robbery
4. Burglary

    5. Vehicle theft
    6. Larceny
    7. Fraud of all types
    8. Rape
    9. Nonviolent sex crime
  10. Narcotics

Allowing five spaces should be sufficient. Multiple listings are often necessary because suspects often don't limit themselves to one offense or one type of offense.

Another field could note whether the person were currently serving time in prison. In this field, it's not necessary to devote space to spelling out yes or no, or to spelling out the name of the prison. A simple code, with a two-digit number for each prison, would do. Leaving the space blank would denote that the person is not currently in prison.

It can also be useful to include fields for items that may be considered partial value judgments, such as the potential for development as an informer or danger to police officers. In some cases, the information will be clear, as in the case of a subject already informing, or someone who has already assaulted or threatened an officer. In others, it will be partly guesswork, but may still be valuable.

A very important field should be devoted to cross-referencing. This should allow enough space for either a name, or a number, or both, depending on how the paper filing system is arranged.

Finally, there's always a need for a general, or miscellaneous, field. This can be entitled "Comments" and hold important information that doesn't quite fit anywhere else.

The foregoing was an outline of a data base used to keep track of persons. It's also necessary to have a data base for keeping track of offenses, listing date and time, nature of offense, incident number, persons involved, disposition, and other data. The basic method remains the same, with fields for each category of information.

Retrieving Data

Quick and convenient access is an important advantage that a data base provides. A bonus is that it's possible to obtain the data in many useful forms. There are several functions involved with data manipulation and access which we should review.

The first is the *Sort* function. The data-base program will accept records entered according to the way the fields are laid out, but once the data is punched in, it's necessary to put it into order. The user has the choice of sorting by any field and in any order he wishes. It's possible to sort alphabetically, by address, or any other field.

The *Find* function is a really useful one. This allows you to find any record according to a set call-out. For example, if it's necessary to find someone named "Smith," the data base will bring up on the screen every record with that name. If it's necessary to have a look at everyone convicted of a sexual offense, the program will bring them up in order. The Find function is a quick way to look for someone who fits a particular picture. This is a very powerful function.

Depending on the type of data base, it may also be possible to search in more than one field simultaneously. It may be possible to search for all Smiths living on Jones Street, for example. This can be a tremendous time-saver, especially when searching for a common name in a very large data base. Instead of scrutinizing all of the Smiths, it's possible to limit the search to Smiths above a certain age, or only the Robert Smiths, for example.

An especially valuable aspect of the Find function is that it may allow searching in any of several different ways, depending on the program. One is the *Generic,* or simple, search. It's possible to find all names that begin with "S," for example, as well as only the "Smiths." If there is doubt regarding spelling, it's also possible to search on the basis of only the first two or three letters. Searching for "Sm" will bring up "Smith," "Smyth," and "Smythe." It will also bring up "Smithson" and longer names as long as they begin with "Sm."

Another way to search for a name, especially when a witness is unsure of both the spelling and the pronunciation, is the *Soundex* search. This brings up all names that sound alike. The *Scan Across* search will seek any alphanumeric combination anywhere in a particular field. An excellent use for this type of search is if a witness remembers only a fragment of a license-plate number. This type of scan will disclose all license plates having that fragment wherever it might be within the number. It can also help you to pick out a telephone number from a fragment or to narrow the search to a manageable number of possibilities.

The final type of search is the *Wildcard* search. One use is when a witness remembers only one or two numbers in a license plate, but is certain that they're in a certain position, such as the beginning or the end. If the witness states that he's sure the plate number ended with a "T," it's possible to bring up all license plates that end with a "T."

The *Printout* or *List* function allows you to make a list or printout of all records that fit a particular set of circumstances. Depending on the data base, it's possible to obtain a printed list of all records named Smith, for example. It's also possible to list all sex offenders under age fifty living in a particular city. The program can make comparisons as well as simple call-outs. Selecting subjects on the basis of age as well as offense is an example of comparison.

What makes this function significantly different from the Find or Search function is that the user can design his own listing format. It may not be necessary to include all of the information available on each subject. If, for example, name, address, and type of offense are enough, the operator can direct the program to list only these on the format.

This selectivity can be very important when generating a list for anyone outside the intelligence office. There may be entries in each record that are not for general dissemination. Rather than go over the printout with a marker pen to cross out the sensitive information, it's more convenient to custom-design the information suitable for release.

Another function is *Clone*. This allows you to create another data base, either for internal use or for use by another agency. This is very much like the List function, but it places the printout on another disk instead of on the screen or paper. A possible use for this function is if another agency requests a list of all persons within its jurisdiction convicted of narcotics offenses, for example.

Exploiting Electronic Power

In the initial stage, setting up a computerized system can be frustrating and disappointing because it requires a lot of keyboarding (typing in the information), and results don't come quickly when only a few records are available for electronic search. Once the data listing is well under way, results will come more quickly and easily, and the initial effort will soon justify itself.

Chapter 9
Evaluation

Evaluation is the critical intermediate step, vital to the separation of the solid information from the garbage. An intelligence evaluator should always do this before any information goes out to clients. Doing so should be an iron-clad rule, because other officers in the department may not be able to evaluate the information properly and may mistake rumor or conjecture for fact.

It will be difficult to enforce this policy in the long run because many high-ranking officers will demand access to raw information, even demanding to know the identity of a source. Make no exceptions to your policy!

The evaluator ranks the likelihood of the information's validity according to the source and the information itself. The military uses an alphanumeric code for this. A report labeled 1-A is from a very reliable source, and the information itself appears solid either because it is internally consistent or because it's confirmed by another source. The police evaluator may want to use his own notation, because the military system isn't completely adaptable for police needs.

Importance

Both source and information are important in the evaluation, but it's also important to evaluate the information's importance.

1. Top in importance is information that is decisive in the prosecution of a major crime. This is information and evidence without which the case could not proceed; for this reason it is worth major concessions if it should be necessary to negotiate with someone for it. The award may be money or immunity from prosecution, but it is worthwhile because of the critical importance of the evidence.

2. The next category is comprised of information that contributes to a major criminal prosecution and/or thwarting of a major crime but is not important enough to justify a major concession. The rule of thumb is that it's not worth giving immunity for a crime more important than the one being prosecuted. Monetary rewards go at prevailing rates.

3. Next in priority is important information that helps fill in the background in a major case, but doesn't contribute to a direct prosecution.

4. The next category is routine information obtained through routine investigation, such as civil or criminal records.

5. The lowest rank is for information that is already widely known on the street. Although true, it's not exclusive or restricted in any way.

Validity

In the same way, we can classify validity of information:

1. At the top is information that appears to be very likely, such as the marital status of the subject of an investigation. In this hypothetical case, the information is supported by statements from neighbors and official records.
2. Next in line is information that's probably true, such as a report of a planned robbery by a gang that has committed such robberies before.
3. Then comes information that is plausible, but impossible to verify or confirm in any way.
4. Below this is information that is improbable, such as a report of someone's acting entirely out of character. All other relevant information contradicts the report.
5. Finally, there is false information, such as a report of a bank robbery planned for a date on which banks are closed.

Reliability of Sources

We can classify the reliability of sources in this order:

1. The most reliable is a source that has proven to be repeatedly reliable in the past. The source can be personal, as with an informer, or impersonal, such as an encyclopedia or other reference work.
2. Next in rank is a source that's usually been

reliable, with an occasional error or ambiguity. The source is in a position to know the information supplied.

3. Below this comes the uncertain source that may or may not be correct. This could be an anonymous letter or phone call. It might also be a statement from a suspect in a crime who attempts to shift the blame to another.

4. Next in rank is the source that's usually wrong. This may be a person who invents "facts" for payment, or who is not in a position to know the information he or she purports to supply.

5. At the bottom is one that's always wrong. This source is, of course, totally unreliable.

The intelligence officer can assign any codes he wishes to these categories for entry into a computer data base. It might be alphanumeric (such as 1-A-1) or totally numeric, such as 1-1-1.

Assessing Information

Assigning codes is easy, but the detailed analyses and interpretations can be very difficult. A good example is a john list that was taken in a raid upon a massage parlor or "dungeon." The officer will see a list of names, almost certainly not in the clients' handwriting, and may be tempted to enter the list verbatim. He also may be amused to find the names of local judges, politicians, and even police officials on the list, and chuckle to himself over their imagined sexual habits.

It is unlikely that clients would provide their real names. On the contrary, they are more likely to give aliases. A client who is a criminal might find it funny to give the name of the judge who sentenced him. On the other hand, if the person is very well known in the community, such as the mayor, it might be impossible for him to give any name other than his own. This is why a john list is hard to categorize. Some items on it may be correct, while other names may be totally fictitious.

A human source may vary in reliability. A snitch may have developed a good relationship with his control officer, but also may, because of a need for money, begin inventing information in his eagerness to please. He may not create information totally, but begin shading his facts.

Processing Is Vital

Raw information, as we've seen, can be worse than useless; it can be misleading. This is why the alert intelligence officer evaluates his information according to a set of criteria in order to help him gauge importance, validity, and reliability.

Chapter 10
Dissemination

The intelligence officer cannot disseminate even processed intelligence indiscriminately. Some types of information, if in the wrong hands, can lead to serious consequences, and it is for that reason that information should be classified into several categories:

1. Top-secret information that will compromise a crucial confidential source;
2. Secret information that will ruin an investigation if revealed;
3. Secret information that may alert a subject that he's under suspicion or investigation; and
4. Confidential information, important to police officers working on a variety of cases, that should not be unveiled outside the department because it would reveal police investigative techniques or otherwise be useful to suspects.

Certain information should never be given out, because the long-term harm will outweigh the short-term gain. In some cases, officers guard information very closely. An example of such an instance is the identity of a snitch. Many officers have their own private snitches, and never reveal their identities to anyone, although they make good use of the information so obtained.

Certain items of information can point to a source. Examples are a transcript of a telephone conversation and an item of information that the subject of the investigation has discussed with only one person, namely the informer. If the subject were to ever find out that the police knew the information he revealed to the informer, the source will be obvious.

Category 1 should never go beyond the intelligence unit because it's so explosive. Categories 2 and 3 should go only to officers directly involved in the investigation and who have something to lose if they compromise the information.

Category 4 information can go to officers in routine roll-call briefings, but with a warning that it must not go outside the department. In this regard, it is important to establish a policy that officers will not discuss cases with the media, referring any inquiries to the press relations officer. The press officer will always clear the details of a press release with the commanding officer of the Criminal Investigation Bureau, or the watch commander, before furnishing them to the media.

Leaked information can be compromising in certain forms. One way to avoid this problem is to "sanitize" the information. The intelligence officer can make a photocopy of the report, blank out sensitive information (such as the identity of a snitch), and make a photocopy of the sanitized version for dissemination. A more effective tactic is to write a new report, extracting only the information relevant to the investigation being pursued. This avoids the danger of releasing collateral information to those who have no need to know.

Chapter 11
Security

It is vital to maintain security because of the consequences of information leaks. As we've seen, the variety of information coming into an intelligence bureau brings with it serious consequences if disclosed. At the very least, there can be embarrassment to innocent people. More seriously, a leak can impede an investigation, ruin the prospects for prosecution, cause a source of information to dry up, or result in death or injury to an informer.

Organizational Security
The basic principle of organizational security is the "need to know," meaning that knowledge, even of seemingly trivial details, should be shared only with those who have a need to know the information. The more people who know a secret, the greater the chance of a leak, be it purposeful or inadvertent.

Need-to-know must be a blanket principle when dealing with any intelligence operation because it is possible to build up a comprehensive picture of an organization and its personnel by gathering a mass of "small" details.

Another important reason for tight security is that an intelligence unit works best when its targets remain unaware of its existence. Many targets will be organized crime figures, who have long criminal careers and who are experienced in resisting police penetration and information-gathering. Many don't even have rap sheets. Normal investigative techniques are almost useless because the criminals know how to blunt the attacks and because they are also well insulated against investigation.

Security, which has many facets, does not just mean that the day-to-day workings of the unit should be kept secret; in fact, the unit's very existence must be kept secret. If normal police bureaucratic procedures dominate the unit, secrecy is impossible. Constant transfers in and out of the unit will produce a large pool of officers in the know, and not all will keep their mouths shut. Another problem is that the more recruits there are, the harder it is to maintain quality. There is also an increased chance of a bad egg slipping in. Ideally, an intelligence unit should have a policy of once in, never out. Though this may be an impossible ideal, keeping turnover low always helps.

Physical separation from any police facility is also helpful, since physical compartmentalization enhances security. This is a much-neglected principle. The New York City Police Department, for example, had for decades maintained its intelligence function inside the Bureau of Special Services and Investigations, or BOSSI. BOSSI has actually been a jack-of-all-trades unit, providing bodyguard services to public officials and visiting dignitaries, as well as performing other special police functions. It has even become political, in a sense, because of its watch upon labor unions. BOSSI also carried out surveillance of left-wing elements from the "reds" of the turn of the century to the student activists of the 1960s. This earned it the name Red Squad. By the 1960s, the name had shortened to the Bureau of Special Services, or BOSS. The intelligence function, as mentioned earlier, went to another unit.

A cover name such as Statistics Office is one way to disguise the real functions of the unit. The most unwise move is to include the word intelligence in the unit's name.

A vital reason for keeping the intelligence unit apart is surveillance. Organized crime figures can put surveillance on police facilities, even photographing police officers entering and leaving. It's important not to discount the prospect of a corrupt officer in the department. While an alert commander can keep a corrupt officer from joining the unit, the unit is vulnerable if housed in police headquarters. A corrupt officer can learn a lot about the unit, its mode of operation, and its targets simply by keeping his eyes and ears open.

One excellent way to disguise the unit is to establish another overt intelligence unit with that title. Such a unit would be concerned with gathering and processing crime statistics and information from open sources, while the real intelligence unit does its work elsewhere. The fake intelligence unit can serve as a contact and conduit for the dissemination of reports to investigating officers in the field.

A weak link can be payroll. Municipal employees who make out payroll checks actually have access to the personnel roster. This means that organized crime figures who develop access to someone in the personnel or payroll office can obtain a list of intelligence employees.

An effective way to cover the existence of an intelligence unit is to establish a cover company in the business district. This should be a complete organization, with a charter or incorporation papers, and a corporate checking account to cover payroll. This allows employees to keep their real duties secret because there's nothing to link them to the police department. The same money-laundering techniques that criminals use can serve to conceal the existence and function of an intelligence unit. In big cities with extensive organized crime gangs, such protective measures are definitely necessary.

Physical Security

Loss of secrecy and physical damage to records are equally severe threats to security. The sensitive nature of the information can destroy an intelligence bureau under some circumstances, and loss of the records can destroy the benefits of years of work. This is why it's vital to safeguard the files against both breaches of security and physical damage.

FIRE PROTECTION

One of Britain's intelligence organizations, the Security Service, also known as MI5, was severely hampered by the destruction by fire of its files in 1939. This was a critical period, and the full effects were not felt for years. Although the Security Service coped very well with German penetrations, Soviet agents had a free run during this time, partly because information that would have aided the search for communist infiltrators was lost in the fire.

Because of the sensitive nature of the information, the usual duplication for storage in a remote vault isn't as satisfactory as it would be for other types of records. Using remote storage means duplicating security arrangements, and budgetary factors often won't allow that additional measure. Instead, the most likely and practical course is to employ maximum security to preserve the main files. This means not only very secure access control, but protection against fire as well. Such protection is vital because fires are so common, as well as being a convenient means by which to dispose of critical evidence and information.

The danger that certain criminal elements will become aware of the sensitive information stored at the site is always present. A gasoline bomb coming through a window can destroy years of work. This calls for definite and thorough security measures:

1. The data storage area should not have windows. Even a barred window can be an entry port for an incendiary bomb or other explosive device. Keeping the data storage area behind interior walls minimizes such a danger.

2. Walls should be fireproofed as much as possible. Carefully choosing appropriate construction materials can help. Brick or block walls retard the spread of fire. While most interior walls are not block, it is possible to rebuild them if the budget allows. If not, a fire-retardant layer could be added.

3. Fireproof filing cabinets are essential. All safes and filing cabinets should have at least a one-hour rating, following Underwriters' Laboratory standards.

4. The computer should be in its own room, with hermetically sealed doors and air conditioning separate from the rest of the building's system.

An automatic fire-extinguishing system is essential. The old water-sprinkler type is very unsuitable for safeguarding records; the best option is a gas system. Many such modern ones use Halon to extinguish fires because this inert gas causes no water damage. There are smoke sensors that respond to the ionization of air caused by smoke. A cigarette will set them off. When the arming relay trips, a horn sounds, giving thirty seconds of warning to evacuate the premises. The system then floods the area with Halon, a nontoxic gas that excludes oxygen from the area.

ACCESS CONTROL

Access control means keeping unauthorized people strictly out of the area. It can't be casual, as with a locked door or a sign saying "Keep Out." People disregard signs constantly, and a locked door is only as good as its lock.

Detectives assigned to the burglary detail can provide information regarding how easy it is to bypass a lock. A pin-tumbler lock will open in seconds to anyone who knows how to use a tension bar and rake. An electronic vibrator gun will buzz open a lock even more quickly. A slam hammer can rip out a tumbler in a couple of seconds. Therefore, it is essential that a serious effort must be made to restrict unauthorized access.

To set up a workable access control system, it's necessary to answer two questions:

1. Will the intelligence bureau be manned twenty-four hours a day or not?
2. Will the unit be located inside the police building, manned twenty-four hours a day?

If the intelligence bureau is within the police building, it should be in the interior, away from windows in order to prevent casual observation, break-ins, and vandalism. In the police station, there's already a certain amount of security because visitors are usually screened and under some sort of restrictions while in the building. It will probably be sufficient to keep the door secured with a combination lock when the office is not occupied.

Having the intelligence unit within the police building presents another problem to security. During working hours, the door to the unit will probably be open, and visitors will wander in. These may be fellow officers who are friends or acquaintances of the people in the bureau. It's important to keep classified material covered when people stroll in.

Some police units shamefully disregard security. In one agency noted for the incompetence of its officers, the very sensitive intelligence function was in an office with an open door, while the public-relations officers kept their office door securely locked during working hours!

In the least secure case—if the unit is in an ordinary office building for cover—it's necessary to be much more careful regarding physical barriers and to give serious thought to keeping the unit manned twenty-four hours a day, every day of the year. It is, of course, preferable to house the unit in a windowless building. If this isn't possible, the offices should be in an interior area of a windowed building.

The outer entrance should open into a lobby, with chairs, tables, and inspection windows made of polycarbonate. This plastic, also known as Lexan, is bullet-resistant. The purpose is to confine visitors (without the oppressive atmosphere of metal bars) until someone can inspect and clear them. The outer door can be very conventional, with an ordinary lock to avoid attracting attention, but the door from the lobby into the work area should be made of steel and have a combination lock or an electronic card lock.

There are some very sophisticated electronic card lock systems that allow a card to be used only once to enter. The card's owner must then use the card to leave before it will gain access again. This occurs in order to avoid pass-backs. Another positive feature of such a system is that the electronic cards gain access only where and when authorized by a central computer that controls the locks. The computer denies access outside of regular working hours to most cardholders and restricts access only to certain areas within the building (each area is partitioned off and has its own door and card lock). These systems are probably too elaborate for all but the largest intelligence units.

If the unit is manned twenty-four hours a day, it's possible to have an electric buzzer lock that is controlled from within. This ensures that no one gets in without being personally identified by someone else, thereby greatly enhancing security without expensive accessories.

It's also important to scrutinize the interior walls and to check out individuals or companies renting adjacent offices. Most interior walls are only studs and wallboard. Being positively flimsy, they can serve as convenient conduits for electronic eavesdropping devices. Anyone aware of the intelligence unit's location can rent an adjacent office and use it as a listening post. Interior walls are also flimsy enough to allow break-ins, because breaking through the wallboard takes only minutes. A steel door at the entrance won't help keep out anyone who uses the interior walls as an access route when the office is unoccupied.

The above considerations make a good case for housing the intelligence unit in its own building, away from other offices. A small building on its own lot provides fairly good security against eavesdropping or break-ins, especially if the lot has a strong fence to discourage unauthorized access.

MAINTAINING PHYSICAL SECURITY

It's vital to control the flow of both police and civilian visitors to the unit. A visitor log helps control traffic, and provides a list of possible suspects if there should be a breach of security. One or more unused offices to serve as interview rooms will help security. It's important that these be actual offices, with a desk and several chairs, rather than the usually blank interview room found in many police facilities. The reason for this is that some visitors will be fellow officers, and it's helpful to promote good relations by a show of hospitality. Relegating them to an obvious interview room might appear antagonistic.

Controlling visitors once inside the unit is also part of the plan. No visitor should be left unattended or unescorted, since such a person could pose a potential security leak. This is not to say that even high-ranking police officers are suspects, but keeping visitors from areas where they might see or hear something unconnected with the purpose of their visit is good security. This follows the need-to-know principle.

There should be an inflexible rule that classified material doesn't go out of the office, since it can become lost, stolen, or copied once off the premises. All classified material should be locked away during lunch hours and breaks. It's too easy for someone to walk in, pick up a paper from a desk, and disappear with it.

At closing time, every employee should secure his or her work area, locking away any sensitive documents. It's best to adopt the widest possible definition of "sensitive documents." A phone number scribbled on a pad can be sensitive if it's the number of an informer.

Another potential security problem comes with discards and wastebaskets. The office should have a shredder, and each person should empty his wastebasket into it before leaving the office for whatever reason. Each person should also be responsible for cleaning his or her work area in order to avoid bringing in cleaning people, who can pose a security leak. The commander should designate a clean-up day at least once a month, during which every employee dusts and vacuums his area.

Many police officers are blind to the danger from trustees. In one case, police officers had trustees load their practice ammunition for them. This offered a splendid opportunity for a trustee who was secretly a cop-hater or who wanted to play a dangerous practical joke to hurt a police officer. It would be surprising if organized crime figures had not already taken advantage of the opportunities presented by police using trustees for menial tasks. Having a member of the organization arrested on a minor charge, such as drunk and disorderly, provides access. Because police select trustees from among those who are serving very short sentences for minor convictions or are awaiting trial on similar charges, a security leak can easily occur.

It is important that everyone in the unit have access to weapons, especially during off-hours and when working alone. This doesn't mean that every secretary must carry a handgun, but only that there must be at least one weapon available in case of emergency. All personnel should, of course, have had basic weapons training, which can greatly enhance the employee's sense of security.

Another problem for intelligence and undercover officers is body armor. The risks of being shot are much less for intelligence and undercover officers compared to members of the patrol force, and this often induces complacency. Moreover, an intelligence officer who plans to spend eight hours in his office isn't likely to want to wear body armor while behind his desk. This is why it's important to know that body armor resembling civilian wear is available in the form of jackets and suit vests. They can be worn when the officer leaves the office, or as needed.

Several manufacturers of plainclothes armor are:

> Point Blank Body Armor
> 55 St. Mary's Place
> Freeport, NY 11520
> (800) 645-4443
> Attn: Tony Borgese

> Second Chance
> P.O. Box 578
> Central Lake, MI 49622-9989
> (800) 253-7090
> Attn: Richard Davis

> Silent Partner
> 612-18 Third Street
> Gretna, LA 70053
> (800) 321-5741
> Attn: Diane Zufle

Police officers have been needlessly injured and killed because they didn't wear body armor even though it was available. Therefore, it should be departmental policy that all officers wear armor whenever possible. A written policy, adequately enforced, will help to avoid or reduce liability. Intelligence officers should don body armor whenever they leave the office. It may be necessary to make occasional exceptions to this policy for certain sensitive undercover operations.

Personnel Security

There are two concerns in personnel security: having an individual officer blown and the corrupt staffer.

An officer can be blown (his identity as an intelligence officer becomes known) if observed at a meeting with an informer. He can also be followed to or from such a meeting, with equally serious consequences.

It's almost impossible to avoid being blown, as it will happen sooner or later. A police officer who's spent time on the street will have made his share of arrests and become known to certain criminal elements. If he is later seen in the company of an informer by someone he has arrested, it won't take a terribly brilliant mind to draw the connection.

The larger the jurisdiction, the less chance of being recognized. However, in some delicate cases, another party in the case may tail an informer. If this party then tails the officer who met with the informer back to the office, the results can be serious. This is why an intelligence officer should maintain his street awareness, always checking for tails. Doing so should be routine practice, since a tail may develop tangentially to his current case or in relation to another case. The moments of maximum danger are when going to and returning from a meeting with an informer and when going to a sensitive location, such as an intelligence bureau office that's undercover in a commercial building. Checking for a tail is part of normal countersurveillance practice.

A less-common problem, but one that causes intelligence and undercover officers much worry, is meeting one of their subjects in a public place with the family present. This is therefore a good argument for selecting only unmarried officers for undercover duty.

The corrupt staffer is another problem, one that's much harder to detect and handle. There are many reasons for corruption, including greed, the need for money to recover from heavy debts, and personal animosity.

Because of the possible consequences that may result when a staffer "turns," the intelligence bureau commander should really know his staff, going beyond the usual screening process for police applicants, both civilian and sworn. Many people feel that nepotism and fraternization are bad words, but following these practices may go a long way toward ensuring loyalty among the staff.

Hiring a qualified relative of a staff member is a safer bet than hiring a total stranger, since there's an additional layer of knowledge about the person that is absent when hiring off the street. The unit commander can have an in-depth view of the candidate that the department's personnel officer is unable to see. This in-depth view comes through familiarity with the family, which is worth more than the usual cursory background check.

Fraternization is the name of the game. Disciplinarians in the police and military frown on this, feeling that it degrades unit discipline. In their view, keeping a distance between a commander and his subordinates is essential to keep subordinates in their place. This is perhaps a useful crutch for a commander with a weak personality; the strong commander builds discipline by building personal devotion.

The strong commander manages his unit without the false status conferred by rank, inspiring his people to obey his orders because of his competence and not by standing on the rules. His managerial style is "follow me" instead of "you go first." He doesn't assign any of his people to jobs that he can't or wouldn't do himself. At the same time, he builds loyalty by making it clear that he views them as his subordinates, not his inferiors.

Fraternization helps keep the commander aware of the aspirations and problems of his subordinates. He may be able to judge when someone is getting into debt, having marital woes, or feeling stalled in his career. These are conditions that sometimes can lead an officer to sell out, and the competent commander can see problems developing, rather than being caught by surprise. He is thus able to have the opportunity to forestall them, instead of letting them develop until they're out of control.

The following are some warning signs of possible problems at the office to watch out for:

1. The person who takes classified work home.
2. The employee who spends an unjustified amount of time at the copy machine.
3. The staff member who puts in excessively long hours, especially when nobody else is in the office. Time alone offers ample opportunity to ransack the files or copy documents.

COUNTERSURVEILLANCE

There is no escaping the threat of surveillance. The likelihood of being watched depends very much on the subjects of the intelligence unit's efforts. Any organized crime ring, whether its main concern is drugs or stolen vehicles, has enough money to pay for very elaborate surveillance.

An organized crime ring can bring in outside talent from another city to provide surveillance agents unknown to local law-enforcement officers. A dummy company or a nearby residence will allow surveillance of anyone who enters the intelligence unit's premises. This sort of discreet surveillance can very quickly result in an album of photographs of intelligence officers. Further surveillance, by means of tails, can disclose whom they meet and where they go. This is why it pays for members of an intelligence unit to know their neighbors. Although they want to retain their low profile, and even anonymity, they need to know who is renting on either side of them or who is occupying premises down the block that offer a vantage point for observation and photography.

A quick way to make a neighborhood survey is for uniformed officers in a marked unit to canvass the block and building. The pretext can simply be a door-to-door investigation, with officers showing renters and residents a photograph from an old file and asking if the person has been seen in the area. This can be one way to start a conversation and elicit additional information regarding the neighbors without giving the appearance of an interrogation.

Intelligence officers also have to keep an eye out for the usual surveillance props, such as a van or camper parked on the street. Such a vehicle makes a good observation post, and a routine step for the police is to check the plate number of every such vehicle in the area through motor vehicle records and the main data base.

Checking for a tail isn't difficult, especially for a police officer. While on foot, it's worth stopping and pausing, looking into a shop window while checking to see if anyone else also has stopped. Walking up an uncrowded block can also disclose a tail.

It is more difficult to discover a team tail than an individual tail because the team member immediately following the subject will not stop; instead he will walk past the subject and let another member pick up the tail. He'll then drop back and rejoin the procession later. Detecting such team tails—and losing them—requires more drastic measures. One tactic is to have a list of buildings with two entrances. Once a tail is detected, the officer can enter by one entrance and immediately leave by means of the other. He can jump into a taxi when no other cabs are immediately available or go into a high-rise and take a crowded elevator. Anyone who jumps in quickly or gets off on the same floor may be a tail. Anyone who takes the same elevator down most certainly is one.

Another way to shake a tail is to use the subway system, if the city has one. Getting on a train and jumping out just as the doors close will often send the tail for a long ride. If there's reason to believe that a team is tailing, getting rid of the entire team will require going to an express stop. Often, both a local and express train are in the station at the same time. Getting off one and running for the other as the doors close will almost surely get rid of the entire team.

For the intelligence officer, shaking a tail isn't the entire story. Identifying the tail is equally important, and in a well-run intelligence unit there should be a contingency plan to cover this eventuality. One way to do so is for the unit member who detects surveillance to immediately telephone the office from the nearest public phone. It's important to use a public phone to avoid the possibility that the phone at his destination may be tapped. The officer being tailed gives the duty officer at the unit a description of the person or persons tailing him, and his own itinerary. This allows the duty officer to send a countersurveillance team to observe the tail. There should be ample opportunity to take surreptitious photographs of the tail, which should be a task of the highest priority if there's more than one person on the tail. Photographs circulated among other members of the unit and such sensitive police details as the narcotics squad can help them detect whether unit members are being followed.

Once the officer being tailed becomes aware that his team has caught up with him, he continues his itinerary until he gets a prearranged signal to shake his tail. Counter-surveillance team members then follow the tail until they discover whom he contacts, where he lives, and who he is. This procedure can reveal an entire surveillance operation and provide positive information about who is running it.

Another expedient measure is to detain a tail. If the tail's using a vehicle, he can be detained without provoking suspicion if a marked unit makes a traffic stop on the vehicle. The traffic stop can actually serve two purposes. One is to obtain information on the tail by examining his ID and that of the vehicle. The other is to allow the officer being followed to proceed unobserved by detaining the tail for a short time, which need be only a few minutes.

It's necessary to have a pretext for a traffic stop in order to avoid arousing the shadower's suspicion that he has himself been blown. If the shadower suspects anything irregular, it will make it much more difficult for the counter-surveillance team to follow him to his destination after the marked unit clears from the traffic stop.

One way for a traffic stop to appear innocent is if the tailing vehicle has a taillight out or is behaving in a way that gives a uniformed officer a plausible reason to make a traffic stop. Countersurveillance team members can determine this by simple observation and call in a marked unit by radio if they feel that it's a workable plan. They can also serve as unobtrusive backups for the officer making the traffic stop, which is important in case the stop suddenly turns hot.

Another way to justify a traffic stop is for the officer being tailed to stop in a place that forces the other vehicle to stop in a restricted or "No Parking" zone. The marked unit then has an excuse to move in and scrutinize the vehicle's occupants.

Yet another way for a unit to stop a following vehicle is for the officer being shadowed to park his car and start walking in a place that will force the pursuer or pursuers to park their vehicle. A member of the countersurveillance team disables the car once the tail is out of sight. The simplest way to do so without causing permanent damage is to let the air out of a tire. The officer leading the parade returns to his vehicle after a few minutes and drives away. The shadowers return to theirs, find it disabled, and are forced to abandon the task. Meanwhile, a marked unit rolls up and the officers inside offer assistance, thereby providing the pretext for checking ID.

As a last resort, it's possible to stop a tail by staging an accident if he is using a vehicle. An unmarked unit serves as a crash car, engaging in a fender-bender with the tailing vehicle. The officer driving must be a very good driver so that he can judge the force needed to cause sheet metal damage without risking human injury. The crash must also take place in a way that doesn't allow the tail to leave the scene of the accident. A marked unit must also be nearby so that it arrives quickly and takes control of the situation without alerting the tail that the crash was intentional or that the occupant of the other car is a police officer.

Alertness Pays
Maintaining security is important, but some officers be-

come complacent after several years on the force. A single breach of security can have serious consequences. This is why it's important for the commander of an intelligence unit to hold regular security briefings and discuss with his staff any security problems that have arisen. Asking for feedback from the staff can help improve security practices and enhance the unit's effectiveness.

Chapter 12
Organization and Personnel

An intelligence unit offers a long-term assignment. It takes time to train and season an intelligence officer. Likewise, it takes time for an officer to build up his sources. This means that an intelligence assignment is not a career-building post. If the department's policy is to rotate officers in assignments every two years or upon promotion, there must be an exception for the intelligence unit because this policy will impede the development of truly competent career intelligence officers.

There must be opportunities for promotion within the unit. This is essential in order to prevent the assignment from being viewed as a dead end for those with limited abilities. Just as importantly, senior officers must not treat the intelligence unit as a dumping ground for misfits. In every department there are misfits against whom superior officers can't write enough paper to dismiss them on charges. The temptation to dump them where the supervisor feels they won't do much harm is sometimes overpowering. The result is often a transfer to press relations, crime prevention, or intelligence. Actually, there are few posts in which a misfit can't do harm, but as long as it's out of a supervisor's area of responsibility, he feels that he's solved the problem. In reality, he has only passed his problem on to another area.

Civilians

An unusual and imaginative approach to staffing an intelligence unit is to develop civilian intelligence officers. For decades, military intelligence was ignoring a large talent pool by limiting posts to military officers. With the need for expansion caused by various wars and a realization that civilians often had much-needed talents that military officers lacked, the integration of civilians became common. Today, intelligence organizations are largely staffed by civilians.

This is also true of the police force; there are some jobs that can best be performed by civilians. Police officers simply don't have all of the skills required to do everything. It's also unnecessary to have an academy-trained sworn officer for many of the posts in an intelligence bureau. Selecting civilians for certain key posts can enhance the functioning of the intelligence unit.

One obvious slot is the typist or keypuncher. In any properly run intelligence unit, there will be a large daily ration of information to enter into the data bases. Classifying and entering this information accurately is a vital task because upon it will depend later retrieval. It's therefore a mistake to think of a keypuncher as some sort of drone. The job demands talent and an alert mind, since the keypuncher must be diligent and conscientious to avoid snarling the system with mistakes.

Command

Command of the intelligence unit is critical. The officer in charge can have any title, but he should report directly to the police chief or his deputy. The commander must have exceptional integrity because of the sensitive nature of his post. He must not be an empire-builder. He also must resist offers from senior officers and their political masters who seek to misuse the intelligence unit to further their own ends. A politician who, for example, uses the police intelligence unit to gather derogatory information against a political rival can be very dangerous. If the commander allows this to occur, he'll become compromised and will be setting the stage for the corruption or destruction of his unit.

Compartmentalization of functions is essential. A very good reason for this is one that rarely appears in print. There may be an occasional blowup because of an intelligence operation gone wrong. There may be charges of abuses of civil liberties, police snooping, and entrapment. The police chief must maintain plausible deniability, which means that he must be able to claim credibly to the public and his political masters that he did not know about the offending activity. This is a crucial point because it's undesirable to have the entire organization take the blame for a limited operation.

Granted, this involves a certain amount of hypocrisy, but it is necessary. There must be a scapegoat, and the person chosen to head the intelligence unit must understand that part of his job may be to take the flak if an operation goes astray or if there's a break in security.

Qualifications of Intelligence Officers

In selecting police officers for the task, it's important to pick officers who are intelligent, imaginative, self-reliant, and honest. Intelligence officers often work with minimal supervision, and this is a golden opportunity for abuses if the wrong type of person is in the post. Security can also be compromised. Selecting officers who are both security-conscious and sophisticated enough to work within the unit is vital.

INTELLIGENCE

Intelligence is a basic prerequisite. In this context, intelligence means more than performance on an IQ test. Paper and pencil skill is only one part of the qualification, and the rest isn't easy to measure. A competent intelligence officer must have better than average judgment, which is hard to define and impossible to measure precisely.

Good judgment means understanding and evaluating situations and drawing the correct conclusions. It means keeping a sense of proportion about both routine and unusual events and assigning priorities correctly.

Good judgment also ties in with a stable personality. It is important for the intelligence officer to keep on an even emotional keel, more so than most police officers. An erratic and unpredictable intelligence officer is not an asset to the bureau.

A certain degree of sophistication is also necessary. The intelligence officer must understand the structure and functions of his targets. He must know, for example, that "organized crime" is not a group of swarthy men with Italian names. Today, members of organized crime can be of any ethnic derivation; they may be outlaw bikers, Anglo-Saxons, or Vietnamese immigrants.

Officers must be mature—in judgment, but not necessarily in years. They must also have the right orientation and not exaggerate the value of civil rights. They must be able to see the big picture, which is that sometimes circumventing the rights of criminals ensures the rights of innocent citizens. At the same time, they must not be "badge-heavy" and trample on people's rights simply because they have the opportunity to do so.

They must be imaginative and understand how to work around the law to get evidence against criminals. These goals require conflicting aims and management techniques, and only intelligent and conscientious officers can do the job effectively. One nuts-and-bolts qualification is to have a set of informers before joining the unit. A competent criminal investigator should have built up a small network of personal informers during his career.

Self-reliance and honesty are important because the officer often works unsupervised.

TECHNICAL SKILLS FOR SURVEILLANCE

These skills are obtainable through on-the-job training or at various seminars conducted by state and federal police agencies. The larger police agencies set up their own courses in shadowing, surveillance, and such technical skills as bugging and lock-picking.

WEAPON PROFICIENCY

Because a skilled intelligence officer does his job without violence, despite the fictionalized popularizations, weapons proficiency is not all that important. The intelligence officer should, of course, maintain his skill by periodic qualification firing, and by attending any plain-clothes survival schools he can.

DISGUISES

Disguises are not often necessary, though there's some need for quick disguises when carrying out surveillance.

Equipment and Communication

The intelligence officer may need a fully equipped departmental vehicle, or he may decide that he's better off with a low-profile, privately registered vehicle that doesn't look like a detective car.

A fully equipped vehicle has most of the communication gear the officer needs. The radio may be fairly simple, a PTT (push to talk) type, or it may be a more sophisticated 800 megahertz trunking radio that switches frequencies to take advantage of dead time on the air, enabling more channels on fewer frequencies.

If the officer elects to use his own car or a specially procured undercover vehicle, he may want a police radio in the glove compartment and a disguised antenna. He may prefer a portable one that he can slip under the seat or into a coat pocket as the situation demands.

A possible problem can arise with a pager. Many departments issue these to their detectives and higher executives, but they should not be mandatory for intelligence officers. If the officer chooses to carry one, he has to choose the type carefully.

There are three types of pagers:

1. The pager that sounds a beep to signal the bearer to call his office or answering service.
2. The pager that displays a number on a screen. The person trying to raise the bearer dials the pager number and then punches in his number at the sound of a tone. This is the number that

appears on the screen and which the bearer calls.

3. The pager that transmits a voice message over its speaker.

The first pager type is discreet, and doesn't give away any information to other parties. The second type, which displays a number, is not very secure if the officer is having a meeting with an informer or other person and is wearing the pager on his belt where the other person can see the number. A number display can be indiscreet, because the number can be recognized by the officer's contact, who may memorize it and call it himself to find out who is on the other end. The third pager type, which has a speaker, can be very harmful to the officer because he may be surprised at any moment by a voice delivering a message that compromises him or another informer. The intelligence officer should not carry the speaker type of pager on his person under any circumstances. He may carry the number display model, but he should keep it in his pocket or under his coat, out of sight, when meeting with an informer.

Chapter 13
Organizational Hazards

While excessive turnover harms the intelligence unit, a small amount is useful. Turnover prompted by retirements and promotions to top administrative posts clears the way for promotion from within, preventing people from going stale in their slots.

Staleness creeps up on the intelligence unit; it is almost impossible to cure once it happens without almost destroying the unit. Staleness shows itself when officers engage in empire-building and have territorial attitudes toward their functions instead of openly cooperating with other officers and sharing resources.

The police executive overseeing the intelligence unit and its commander needs to know how to determine whether or not the unit is performing effectively and the people within it are doing their jobs. This task requires very clear thinking based on some practical experience.

A serious danger is that the intelligence function can serve as a refuge for the lazy or incompetent officer, the sort known as a "bullshitter," who knows how to curry favor from his superiors while avoiding doing any real work. Another problem arises when a police administrator uses the intelligence officer slot as a reward for loyalty, allowing the person he appoints to use it as a sinecure.

What increases this danger is the fact that it's hard to measure the effectiveness of the intelligence officer or unit by the standards applicable to other police specialties. It's possible to measure effectiveness of traffic officers by the number of citations they write, the quality of their accident reports, or direct observation. There are also norms for case-clearing by criminal investigators. Intelligence officers, however, don't write citations or clear cases, which makes evaluating their effectiveness much more difficult.

The first step, as we've already seen, is good personnel selection. A good guide to present and future performance is past performance. A police administrator who puts the department's misfit into the intelligence slot is only transferring his problems.

Supervision in the normal sense is impossible. Most of the time, the intelligence officer makes his own hours because his is not a nine-to-five job. Policy may require him to maintain a time sheet to account for his hours. He may have to meet an informer late at night and allow himself compensatory time off the next day. If departmental policy allows it, he may award himself compensatory time-and-a-half for the late-night meeting.

A written report on the results of that meeting can be expected. This supports any other claims he may make, such as a mileage chit if he uses his own car or a bar or restaurant receipt.

Working with informers requires an expense account, and this is an opportunity for abuses. A poorly chosen officer may see the expense account as an opportunity to live the high life while someone else picks up the tab. There are several possible controls for this sort of behavior. The first is to check the officer's expense statements against those of the officer who previously worked the slot, and to question any sudden increases. Another control is to check meticulously every claimed expense against the officer's time sheet and other reports to ensure that the expense was warranted. Yet another control is to set up a fixed expense allowance and advise the officer that any excess will have to come from his own pocket. This sets a limit on claims that an informer insisted on being wined and dined at the most expensive restaurant in town.

Another index of performance is record keeping and reports. The superior should regularly read the reports and periodically request reports based on the intelligence officer's records. The intelligence officer should, for example, be able to produce a list of all offenders on parole within his jurisdiction. He should also be able to produce a list of crimes committed in his jurisdiction by category and month.

In this crucial area, the real test is the superior officer's judgment, because evaluating written reports isn't as easy as it seems. An intelligence officer may keep detailed and meticulous records of meaningless information, and a superior officer who scans them uncritically may be convinced that the officer's doing a terrific job. On the other hand, some intelligence officers are very poor in their record keeping because they keep it all in their heads, but may be very effective in spite of this. This type of officer can deliver a thorough and well-organized verbal briefing on his subject even though he can't organize it as well on paper. In a larger intelligence unit, it's possible to employ both types of officers usefully by assigning them to areas where their methods of working are compatible.

The experienced supervisor learns how to recognize the report written just to pad a file. Some officers develop the skill to write reports that are substantially empty but which impress superior officers. This is a hazard in any agency that requires written progress reports whether or not there's anything to report, but it's a particular waste of time in an intelligence unit. If such reports are required by departmental policy, it may not be possible to change the practice unless the superior officer is high enough within the department to do so.

The output of the intelligence officer doesn't consist merely of keeping files. He should be able to help criminal investigators when they need information. When an agency has an effective intelligence officer, other investigators learn to rely upon him for background information and perhaps even some investigative leads. This builds a trusting relationship between the intelligence officer and others and stimulates mutual cooperation because other officers can see tangible benefits from the information they furnish the intelligence officer.

In that regard, the ability to get along with others is vital for intelligence officers. It's not the only quality required, of course, but it is very important. Some people have a knack for fostering personal relationships because they are outgoing and charming, while others don't have such skills, but manage to get along in their jobs nevertheless. There is little danger that a charming intelligence officer will build a reputation based on personality alone without following through with solid production. Police officers deal with deceivers daily and quickly learn to spot a phony.

Using a public office for private purposes is not only corrupt, it's dangerous. The intelligence unit commander who serves his political master in this way leaves himself open to extortion and blackmail because an unscrupulous politician can threaten to expose him. He is also vulnerable if an outside party discovers the affair. The target of a politically motivated investigation will understandably be angry and vengeful. A fast-stepping politician can easily deny the charges, but a police administrator is often left holding the bag. A mini-Watergate can destroy an intelligence unit.

Glossary

Agent in place. An informer or someone who remains in his role with a criminal syndicate or operation while providing information or other services to law-enforcement agencies.

Agent provocateur. From the French *agent provocateur,* this term applies to an agent who stimulates the commission of a crime. Using an agent provocateur is often considered entrapment.

Bust-out. A fraud game in which an organized crime ring buys into or buys out an established firm having a good credit rating and orders material that it immediately resells. The end comes when the company can't pay for the material it has bought, and it then collapses. Creditors are left holding the bag while the ring members have stolen and sold material with a cash value far beyond their initial investment.

Chop shop. A wrecking yard where stolen vehicles are cut up for parts.

Collateral information. Information obtained as a sidelight to another action or investigation. Exploiting collateral information makes for greater law-enforcement efficiency.

Defector. An informer who "comes over," such as the various mob figures who told their life stories to federal agents after entering a protection program.

Flake. Synonym for *plant*. This word comes from the expression "fell on him like a snow*flake*."

Informant. A person, otherwise unconnected with a crime or criminal, who provides information. An informant can be a victim or a witness.

Informer. A person who provides criminal information. This person differs from an informant in that he has more than a casual relationship with the crime or criminal.

Plant. To plant is to place evidence, such as contraband, on a subject's person or premises so that the arresting officer may find it during a search. To do so is strictly illegal, but some unscrupulous officers still continue the practice. A variant is to tell a subject that incriminating evidence has been found in order to entice a confession, a practice that is on the borderline of legality.

Raw information. Information not processed or evaluated.

Shadow. Synonym for tail.

Snitch. Synonym for an informer.

Squeal, squealer. Underworld derogatory term for an informer.

Tail. A tail, used as a noun, is a person (or persons) who surreptitiously follows a subject; as a verb, it refers to the action of following a subject.

Twist. A coercion, threat, or other inducement used to persuade a subject to cooperate. The twist could be in the form of a threat to arrest the subject if he doesn't provide information or a promise to reduce a charge in return for cooperation.

Endnotes

Chapter 1. An Historical Look

1. Christopher Andrew, *Her Majesty's Secret Service* (New York: Viking, 1985), 19.

Chapter 5. Informers

1. Burt Rapp, *Undercover Work* (Port Townsend, WA: Loompanics Unlimited, 1986), 111-114.

Chapter 6. Undercover Officers

1. Burt Rapp, *Undercover Work* (Port Townsend, WA: Loompanics Unlimited, 1986), 34.

Chapter 7. Surveillance

1. Burt Rapp, *Shadowing and Surveillance* (Port Townsend, WA: Loompanics Unlimited, 1986), 21-23.